THE EYE OF ADOPTION

the true story of my turbulent wait

for a baby

Jody Cantrell Dyer

ISBN-10: 1481040138
ISBN-13: 978-1481040136

Bible verses quoted within are from the following versions:

Front cover photograph obtained from fotolia.com

Back cover artwork by Houston Dyer

Cover design by Sherri B. McCall

To

Mark Akers,

a steadfast, seaworthy witness to God's devotion
throughout the adoption voyage

For

Kerri,

my soul sister

THE EYE OF ADOPTION

the true story of my turbulent wait

for a baby

Jody Cantrell Dyer

No One "Just Adopts"

Hope deferred maketh the heart sick:
but when the desire cometh, it is a tree of life.

—Proverbs 13:12

When I was a toddler, I entertained relatives by singing this little song:

Special, special, I am very special
God made me this way!

I would draw out the word "way" as "waaaaaaaaaaay" like an operatic trill, a crowd-pleasing ending to my parlor trick performance. That song rings true for every child. My children are no more special than your children or the child for which you pray and wait. However, adoption *is* special. It was divinely designed and serves as a living example of God's graceful, abundant love for humankind.

I have two friends who, years ago, placed babies for adoption. Each was in college when she was surprised by a crisis pregnancy. One friend told me her experience when she found out my husband Jeff and I were trying to adopt. She gave me crucial advice regarding the birthparents' extended family. Her help later proved vital. The other friend is unaware that I know she placed a baby for adoption. When she sees us, she asks to hold my child. I think holding my baby gives her assurance and peace about the decision she made so many years ago.

My initial purpose in writing this book was to chronicle the sweet and sour elements of our adoption story for my children. I am a public school teacher, not a writer, but I wanted my children to understand the extremes to which their father and I suffered and succeeded to create our family. Our children will have a colorful, descriptive, documented account of a story that tested love, endurance, commitment, and faith, a story they can learn from and someday pass on to their families.

As I revisited my journal entries, mined through letters and emails from friends and relatives, and studied countless pieces of medical documents and adoption paperwork, I realized that my story could benefit people outside my little family. For that reason, I expanded the book to reveal details regarding every step my husband Jeff and I took toward our second child. In these pages I will candidly present information to intimately describe how Jeff and I clumsily but successfully battled through the uncontrolled currents of infertility and adoption.

To protect my adopted child's most personal history, I kept much of the birth family's biological and social background information private. My intention in writing this book is not to expose my child, but to expose the raw and rewarding aspects of adoption.

Throughout each section of this book, I divulge friends', relatives', and strangers' commentary, support, criticism, and reaction. I share the effects of all of the above on my marriage. I also try my best to illuminate God's concern and involvement in every moment of our trek toward a baby.

I hope my story will benefit people who wish to become adoptive parents, regardless of where they are in the process. Whether you decide to adopt after failed fertility treatments, lost pregnancies, a lost child, no chance of conceiving, have a dozen children already, or feel "called" to adopt, I respect you. No matter the circumstances, adoptive parents share a special bond. I hope "waiting parents" will relate to my emotions, experiences, tribulations, and triumphs. I hope by doing so, you find camaraderie, relief, and optimism.

Because adoption is a spiritual transaction conducted within a commercial industry, success in adoption requires involvement from what seems like everyone connected to the adoptive parents. Thus, adoptive parents' friends, relatives, co-workers, and even pets will find themselves here, too. I urge anyone connected to waiting parents to read my story to empathize with the adoptive family and perhaps alleviate, not complicate, the inevitable burdens. Do not underestimate the depths of suffering and lengths of endurance required of adoptive parents. Do not underestimate the difficult choice to find a child through adoption. No one "just adopts."

My mother thought of the book's title, The Eye of Adoption. She has a particular gift for naming pets; my aunts, uncles, and cousins often contract her to name their animals, so I asked her to name this book. After reading the book, her critter-naming gift prevailed once more.

Adoption *is* a storm of faith, fear, paperwork, people, hurt, healing, words, work, devotion, divinity, rawness, revelation, days, and, hopefully, a delivery.

I was not strong on my own. I relied on my husband, my mother, my friends, my family, and my faith to prop me up during my doubtful and weak moments.

I hope my story is a clear window through which you can visualize your potential adoption experience. I hope my story comforts you as you live in the eye of adoption.

The best laid schemes o' Mice an' Men
Gang aft agley,
An' lea'e us nought but grief an' pain,
For promis'd joy!

—Robert Burns, "To A Mouse"

The Master Plan

Do not squander time for that is the stuff life is made of.

—Benjamin Franklin

Though I am a "lonely only" child, I have nine first cousins who enjoy close relationships with their siblings. As a child I did not particularly want a brother or sister. I relished the one-on-one attention and communication I had with both of my parents. They talked with me and included me: we enjoyed a tight bond. When I was nineteen, my father died. It was June 1993. He was forty-four. I had just finished my freshman year of college.

My father's death altered my way of thinking. I suddenly grasped the quantitative nature of my and my mother's existence, life's fragility, and death's finality. I, erroneously, felt responsible for my mother's well being. From then on, I longed for a sibling. I desperately needed a brother or sister, someone who knew exactly how I felt, someone with whom I could commiserate. Also, already known for my smart mouth (a high school teacher nicknamed me "tongue-lasher") my sarcasm and cynicism sharpened.

A week after my father's death, I applied for a summer job at IHOP in Pigeon Forge, Tennessee. My cousin Toby, a return summer worker, championed my cause and implored the restaurant manager to grant me a coveted breakfast shift so I could be home at night with my mother. I did my best to model southern hospitality as I teased customers who ordered the Rooty Tooty Fresh 'N Fruity pancake platter, but grief and anxiety accumulated like the plates precariously stacked up my left arm. Often, when I was exhausted from my trancelike trudge through a day of waitressing, I fibbed to customers when they ordered desserts, "We are out of that." I just wanted the giddy *tourons* (my father's term: half tourist, half moron) to pay and go back to their hotels so I could go home and be miserable with my mother. The fry cooks felt sorry for me and routinely treated me to rich chocolate chip pancakes with hot syrup, Cool Whip, and vanilla ice cream.

In August, I took my plumped up rear and sour attitude back to The University of Tennessee's Humes Hall filled with carefree co-eds. College and the future took on new meaning for me. I became an impatient control freak, worrier, and planner. I wrote papers the same day professors assigned them. If my mother did not answer her home phone, I freaked out, figuring she had died of a heart attack like my father, had a freak accident (she did almost run over herself once), choked on peanuts.... My mind went into orbit with any hint of mystery as to her well-being.

I set my sights on graduating early to save my mother, a high school English teacher, money. I majored in finance to secure a lucrative job; if I became a young widow like my schoolteacher mother, I would be better able support my family. I mapped out my entire future: graduate early, earn a high income, take care of my mother, find a husband, have a big family, and hit all my goals in case *I* was going to die in my early forties. At nineteen, I had already made the decision to have three children when I got married.

Blueprints for Footprints

In dreams begins responsibility.

—William Butler Yeats, *Responsibilities*

Jeff and I married on April 15, 2000. What a deadline. I was twenty-six, and he was thirty-six. We were not naïve. As an only child whose mother suffered two miscarriages, I did not take pregnancy for granted. I sincerely hoped to become pregnant as soon as possible. I even promised my mother-in-law! I wanted those three children.

Jeff and I lived in a one-level, three bedroom ranch home with a flat backyard and a big kitchen. It was in the perfect proximity to hospitals, libraries, and parks. I saw no reason to move until we had a school-aged child. But Jeff wanted to move. That was one of our first *lengthy* arguments. Jeff put a For Sale by Owner sign in the front yard. Daily, after Jeff backed out of the driveway and turned out of sight, I jerked the sign up from the grass and threw it in my backseat. When I got home from work, I pushed it back into place so he would never know. Weeks later, overcome with guilt, I admitted my crime. My forgiving husband hired a realtor to find us a house, so I stuck the For Sale by Owner sign in the grass and left it. Not long after that, I negotiated the sale to a co-worker. So, just four months after Jeff and I married we began looking for a new home in Knoxville.

Jeff wanted to move closer to his friends and be in the "right" school zone. My parents raised me in Sevier County in East Tennessee on seventy-two acres of Appalachian hills, hollers, and creeks. I could see Mount LeConte from my Gatlinburg-Pittman High School parking lot. My mother (who taught at my high school) and I drove through the Great Smoky Mountains National Park every day on the way to and from school. Sevier County has grown tremendously, but when I was growing up, trips to the grocery store, school, hospital, or church were long and tiresome. As a new wife and habitual worrier planning a three-child family, I desired a safer, more convenient location in which to raise my family. My must-haves were much more specific than Jeff's: in *my* search, I combined my future children's needs and my desire to re-create my best childhood memories. I thought through the details and played out all kinds of scenarios. My children needed to grow up close to a hospital. All the bedrooms had to be together so, in case of fire, I could grab my bra (The Red Cross does not usually get my size over-the-shoulder-boulder-holders in their donation bags) and my children and "head for the pines" for safety. I wanted to be able to wash dishes *and* watch my children shoot basketball. My cousin Claire says you know you are in East Tennessee when someone misses a rebound and the ball rolls fifty feet downhill and then a fight ensues about who is responsible for its retrieval: the shooter or the rebounder. We also needed a spot for spinning Big Wheels. I grew up in a one hundred year-old farmhouse, so I was low maintenance. I was not picky, just specific.

Our realtor found several pretty houses near Jeff's friends, but the homes either had split bedrooms or no basketball goal within kitchen view. No deal.

My in-laws lived in Knoxville at that time, so our plan was to stay with them during the old house sale and new house purchase gap. One Sunday, I had had it. Married only a few months and not too eager to live with my in-laws, I decided to rush the process. Jeff was playing at least eighteen holes of golf that morning, so I took off on my own to find a house. I started at Kingston Pike, the main thoroughfare that juts through Knoxville, and took roads left and right until I happened upon a realtor open house in Glen Cove subdivision. Lyons Bend, the road just before Glen Cove, reminded me of Gatlinburg's steep, snaking, sun-dappled roads. I was still unfamiliar with that area of Knox County. Having driven in *all* directions *all* morning, and being naturally "spatially challenged," I thought I was out in the boonies but went in anyway. I was surprised when the realtor informed me that youth baseball fields and Lake Loudon were only a half-mile away. She further explained that Glen Cove was zoned for Jeff's sibling's old elementary school, and was only a few miles from our church. The house was ten minutes from the UT campus, ten minutes from Children's Hospital, and two miles from Food City.

The 1956 basement rancher contained three bedrooms all on the northern edge of the house and a large guest room with its own bathroom and sunroom on the southern edge of the house. I could store my children on one end and my mother on the other! The basement–just a huge playroom–was a bonus. The Poplar and pine-shaded backyard offered a safe place for children to explore. The sunny, sloped, grass-covered front yard was ideal for a Slip-n-Slide. The back patio, my favorite spot, was the perfect place to spin figure eights on a Big Wheel. Best of all, when I stood at the kitchen sink, I looked out the window to see a basketball goal, slap in the middle of the backyard.

I called Jeff and exclaimed, "I found our house! You need to come over here right now." I stood guard at the open house until it was over, making small talk with the listing agent and shooing away any other lookers. When Jeff arrived, I used every ounce of my newlywed allure, wit, and equity and took advantage of his eighteen-hole beer buzz to sell him on the house. He agreed to make an offer. I called our realtor. He came and we drew up a full offer contract.

When Jeff and I got home, we talked about our new house. He asked, "How big was that garage?" I told him there was not one. I had whisked him through that house and completely manipulated the deal but it was too late then. I was determined to have that house; the location and the important things—to me—were there. Within days, our full-price offer secured for us a wonderful place to raise our three children. We stayed with Mr. Dyer (Mrs. Dyer was visiting Jeff's brother, who was working in Africa at the time) for three weeks. Each afternoon, Jeff and I would leave work, go to his parents' house and change clothes, and then go to Glen Cove to pull up filthy, decades-old carpet, score and strip cigarette-smoke stained wallpaper, and paint. Jeff's daddy (also named Jeff) brought us supper almost every night. When Mrs. Dyer returned from Africa, she bragged on our remodeling work but admonished us for our combined fifteen-pound weight gain. Jeff and I moved to Glen Cove.

In May 2001, when we had been married a year, Jeff's sister Jenny came to Knoxville to visit for Mother's Day and Jeff's birthday. Coincidentally, Jeff's birthday fell on Mother's Day that Sunday, May 13th. The Friday night before, Jenny announced to all of us that she was pregnant with her first child. Thrilled for her, I was sad for me. I had been trying to become pregnant since my wedding day, and I was getting worried. I happened to be a few days late in my cycle and had actually stopped at CVS to buy a pregnancy test. After hearing Jenny's big news, I over-celebrated slash self-medicated with a few vodka tonics, forgetting until just before I went to bed that I had a pregnancy test in my purse. With liquid courage, I went into the bathroom, took the test, and waited the three minutes.

I was shocked to see two pink lines appear. I looked at that little stick, expecting that second pink line to fade away, but it remained. I was pregnant! I stared at the test for a moment, then walked into our bedroom and told the always-calm Jeff I was pregnant.

He responded, "Are you sure? Take another one in the morning."

He was hesitant. I was elated. Saturday morning, I tested positive again. Jeff and I smiled and savored the momentous revelation all day.

Sunday morning, we attended church with Jeff's family and celebrated Mother's Day and Jeff's birthday with brunch on the Dyer's back porch. Jenny was happily babbling about her big news. Jeff and I, still in shock, mentioned nothing about ours. Women's intuition never fails. Halfway through the meal, Mrs. Dyer looked at me and asked, "Jody, how long have *you* been pregnant?" I delighted in this once-in-a-lifetime opportunity.

"About three weeks."

Screams of delight filled the patio; we sounded like the bird exhibit at the Knoxville Zoo.

I visited my gynecologist the next morning. He tested my hormones. My progesterone levels were quite low so he prescribed vaginal suppositories. I had to insert the progesterone "tubes" at 7:00 a.m. and 7:00 p.m. each day and lie still for thirty minutes after each insertion. I was a bank branch manager in downtown Knoxville at the time. We had these ridiculous weekly "call nights" each Thursday. From 6:00 p.m. to 8:00 p.m. we phoned customers and tried to set appointments to sell bank products. To accurately maintain my 7:00 p.m. suppository schedule on those nights, I sneaked to the ladies room two floors beneath my office, near the hefty main vault filled with hundreds of safe deposit boxes.

I inserted the medicine and laid flat and still (there are no pillows in bank basements) for thirty minutes, just as the doctor instructed, praying my male boss did not ask where I was. God was looking out for me because, for the six weeks in a row I did drugs in the vault, my boss never caught on. Other than that, my pregnancy was healthy and surprisingly easy; I never threw up, and I had no issues that I knew of other than low progesterone.

Just days before Christmas, Jenny gave birth to my precious niece Ellie.

On January 7, a week before my due date, I visited my obstetrician. I begged her to induce me the next day. She agreed. I was so keyed up, I mistakenly took the wrong Interstate 40 ramp and drove miles out of my way before I realized I was headed to Nashville. I went home, called the bank human resources department and my boss to tell them I was beginning my maternity leave. I called my mother who squealed in delight. She planned to stay with us the first week after I gave birth.

My matchless mother, a hyper-thinker, has mastered the art of anticipation. She loves to make lists and pack coolers (a throwback to her University of Georgia days of partying) and suitcases. She had packed her bags, made a list of suppers and treats she would cook for Jeff and me, and purchased birth announcements, stamps, and envelopes. She was ready to be a grandmama! On the phone, she told me she had cleaned and ironed a particular bold-colored shirt so her infant grandson would "immediately notice" her. She hung up the phone and carried her suitcases to the driveway. She carefully draped the outfit over her suitcase and went to make sure the stove was off and to lock the front door. Then, in a typical fit of excitement, she cranked up the car and backed over her own suitcase. When my frenzied mother got to my house, she showed me her black shirt, embellished with large, bright puppy faces and muddy brown tire tracks.

The next afternoon, family and friends eagerly waited at Fort Sanders Hospital on The University of Tennessee campus for the arrival of Jefferson Houston Dyer III. At 5:21 p.m., January 8, 2002, Houston was born.

Jeff walked into the waiting room to a crowd of Houston fans and proudly announced, "He looks just like me."

The Enemy: Infertility

A whippoorwill on a window still-
it should have made me smile
But everything sounds lonesome to a melancholy child

—DiPiero & Tillis, "Melancholy Child"

That year I turned 28 in February and Jeff turned 39 in May. Aware of our progressing ages and my master plan, we had no time to waste. I began trying to conceive our second child in October of 2002, when Houston was only nine months old. The annoying things I had to endure with pregnancy were minor compared to what was coming.

As a child, I loved hearing the story of my mother's pregnancy. Birth stories are full of happiness and gratitude with unique details that make children feel loved. While my mother was pregnant with me, she and my paternal grandmother Wimmie began writing journals for me.

Throughout my pregnancy, I kept a journal for Houston detailing my and Jeff's excitement, plans for Houston's future, and how much we already loved him. I daydreamed on paper.

I kept a journal for "Baby #2" but in a much different format for many reasons. Initially, I used the journal to vent my frustrations and record efforts in the fertility battle.

During that time, Jeff and I happily welcomed our lively niece, Anna Kate. I loved being an aunt. My desire for another child intensified.

For two years, I used ovulation kits and timed our love life. When trying to conceive my second baby, I spent a couple of years in denial. I reconciled that, since my first pregnancy went so smoothly, I would soon be pregnant. I blamed the negative results on Jeff's being out of town for business, my misreading ovulating kits, my diet, and everything imaginable and reasonable. I also blamed my infertility on my stressful job. I worked hard, but I was consumed with trying to conceive. I was a mother to toddler Houston and an extremely busy branch manager, so I kept one fat daily appointment book. Once, a male co-worker glanced at the open book on my desk and innocently asked, "Why do you have a heart drawn on Thursday?"

I bluntly admitted, "That's when I ovulate so Jeff and I have to have sex that night." He blushed, left, and never looked at my planner again.

In December 2004, I quit my job as a bank branch manager in hopes that the lower stress lifestyle of a housewife would help me conceive. Jeff had switched from a career in sales to become a realtor and could support us on his own. The change in lifestyle definitely made life with Jeff and a three-year-old Houston more enjoyable, but, sadly, being a stay-at-home mother did nothing to boost my fertility. Houston was potty-trained, and I was utterly frustrated. I sought help from a specialist. Our first appointment cost $1,900.00. We rapidly used up money and months. Two months into treatment, I jokingly threatened the doctor, "If I'm not pregnant in six months, I'm going to start smoking. If I'm not pregnant in a year, I'm doing meth. Smokers and drug addicts get pregnant all the time. You don't want that on your conscience. The pressure is on, doctor." Jeff and I answered awkward questions and endured embarrassing procedures for the next four years. A friend teased Jeff, "I hear you've been treating your body like an amusement park."

Below is an excerpt from my Baby #2 journal, dated August 8, 2006, two years into the fertility treatment trials.

> *Dear Hopefully Baby #2,*
>
> *I've been trying to have you for four years now! No luck but a big effort this week should help. My fertility doctor performed hysteroscopy, laparoscopy, and dilation and curettage. He said he could barely identify my reproductive organs; they were encased in scar tissue, likely a result of my birth defect, gastroschisis. He diagnosed me with a clotting disorder (MTHFR). He said I have been pregnant two or three times since Houston and wrote in the post-op report, "There is no rational explanation for the patient's previous pregnancies." That includes Houston! I am hoping for another miracle. Am I selfish? I am emotionally, physically, financially, and mentally exhausted but I feel you are on your way to me somehow. I will do everything I can to make you, my dream of a baby, real.*
> *I love you,*
> *Mama*

I include that letter not to dredge up pity but to remind readers that the devastation of infertility is a monthly cycle fraught with anxious anticipation and gut-wrenching disappointment.

I kept a detailed log of ovulation, menstruation, and sexual activity for my doctor. I hated the necessary invasion of privacy.

By this time, Jeff's parents had moved back to Nashville, which meant a three hour drive and usually an overnight visit for us. I swear on the Smoky Mountains, for years it seemed like every time we visited them, no matter where I was in my cycle, I either ovulated, which meant I had to skip that month of trying (I could never have sex in the same house as my sweet in-laws—gross) or I spontaneously menstruated, which meant I had to suffer another round of disappointment without the needed privacy for my monthly crying jag.

I actually carried pregnancy tests to Nashville with me. Once when I started my period there, I had a meltdown. In a tantrum, I took Jeff's car keys and my pity-party attitude to Walgreens Drug Store. I stomped through the store to find the feminine hygiene/family-planning aisle. I bought the biggest boxes of tampons and pads I could find, thinking, *Okay God, I just spent twenty-five bucks on supplies; if the laws of biology won't help me, maybe Murphy's Law will!*

Throughout my years of trying to conceive, I took sixty-five pregnancy tests. They were all negative.

Friends and family should not underestimate how such a systematic dose of failure hurts. I spent six years, wasted thousands of dollars, and humiliated my husband and myself trying to have a second child while people all around me easily became pregnant—or so it felt to me.

I suffered bouts of anxiety and depression, often related to high doses of hormones and fertility drugs. I wrestled self-doubt, weight gain, poor self-esteem, mood swings, and bitterness toward pregnant people.

To battle the hormone and depression-induced bulge, I exercised almost daily. I would drop Houston off at school and head to Lakeshore Park, near our house. The park contains flag football and the previously mentioned youth baseball fields, as well as a two-mile walking trail. Ironically, the park surrounds Lakeshore Mental Health Institute.

I felt pretty "mental" as I paced around that track each morning. For a long time, I took heavy doses of Clomid and progesterone. I never felt suicidal, but I was *down*. Because I took such strong doses of medicine, I understand the mind-altering power of drugs. I remember walking across roadways during my exercise routine, leering at oncoming cars, and not really caring if they hit my bloated blubber butt. My melancholic attitude only worsened as I plodded past skinny, fit, young mothers jogging behind their babies' strollers.

Small Talk

Dispute not with her: she is lunatic.

—William Shakespeare, *Richard III*

When you are a young married woman and/or a young mother small talk often surrounds the topic of family planning, so by this point friends and acquaintances knew that I was trying to get pregnant. I hated baby showers, and when I did go to one, I usually cried all the way home. I dealt with all kinds of remarks and "advice." I would be sitting at the pool with a bunch of mothers watching our boys do pencils and cannonballs off the diving board or I would be downtown Knoxville eating lunch with my work buddies, and the topics of children, parenting, or having more children would arise.

Inevitably someone would say to me, "Just stop trying and it will happen." Depending on my mood or hormone level, I either gently replied, "Oh, you are probably right" or curtly responded "If I don't have sex when I am ovulating, I will not get pregnant. I have to *try*."

I truly despised the comment "Just relax and you will get pregnant."

I tried to bite my tongue, but my usual reply was, "I'm not sure I can relax that right fallopian tube out of a medical waste facility and back into my body, functioning properly!" Another thoughtless comment that an early obstetrician made was, "Just go to Victoria's Secret and buy something sexy." Even if Victoria's Secret did sell negligees large enough to contain my Dollyesque boobs, it could not fix my problem. I despised the comment, "Wow, I just look at my husband and I get pregnant." Perhaps I should have replied, "Well, I've looked at your husband, and I still don't see how *you* got pregnant!" My fertility specialist said people mean well but cannot relate and just want to say *something*.

Another statement I endured pretty often during fertility treatments *and* the adoption process was, "Just be thankful you have Houston." Really?

One should never feel selfish for wanting another child. I wanted a sibling for Houston. I felt Houston wanted a sibling. In retrospect, I think the pains of infertility and later adoption trek only amplified my love and appreciation for Houston, and likely made me a better parent to him. I slowed down and enjoyed Houston's unique personality, moments of soulful abstract thinking, and comical stunts.

Men and women who are seeking to be parents for the first time, through infertility or adoption, have my sincerest empathy. During my "low tides," I often reminded myself, *At least I am a parent and get to enjoy the life-altering and life-enhancing experience of simply being someone's mother.* I felt (feel) acutely sorry for those struggling to *begin* a family, and I pray this book is a comfort to them. "Childless parents"—as I like to call them—deserve elite prayer and extraordinary consideration.

Sweet Offers and Great Sex Advice

I wanna baby, I can't explain it,
it's like being hungry or having to pee.

—Elinor Lipman, *Then She Found Me*

During that somber time, many friends and family members showed kindness and concern. My cousin, Annie, offered to be a surrogate mother for me. I was not a candidate, and we could not afford surrogacy, but I will never forget her incredibly kind gesture. Over and over, I opened up to friends and family about my struggle. In response to a prayer request email I sent out, my cousin Claire wrote, "I always pray for my cousins but I'll be more specific! Have you tried Robitussin?"

The battle with infertility can get gruesome. Some women take Robitussin because it helps thin the cervical mucus so the sperm can swim through the rigorous reproductive channel with less difficulty. I tried Robitussin, and I blamed Jeff, of course, when that did not work. I told him his sperm must be putting on a synchronized swimming show because they were obviously playing around with no sense of urgency toward the target.

My cousin Toby said that she had a friend who became pregnant after years of trying when alone she repeatedly yelled "Devil, get out of my life!" I wonder how I looked, driving down Kingston Pike, hopped up on Robitussin, screaming at the devil.

The funniest advice I received came from Jeff's cousin Meleia. She told me that, after Jeff and I had sex, I should immediately lean my legs straight up against the wall. She said gravity would get the sperm going in the right direction. I hate to admit that I followed her advice, but I tried anything and everything I thought would help me. So, for many months, after each time we, well, you know, I quickly spun around in the bed, stuffed pillows under my rear-end to create an inclined plane, threw my size nine feet up on the wall, and, in the spirit of Dory and Nemo, chanted in my head, *Just keep swimming. Just keep swimming!* For Jeff's sake and to preserve some dignity, I always grabbed a quilt and covered the rest of me.

One night, just as I was performing my baby-making gravity routine, a car drove by our house. Suddenly, it dawned on me that my Glen Cove neighbors could be getting a free show. Our bed has no headboard; it is pushed up under an eighty-inch wide window that looks out over our sloped front yard, which overlooks the entrance to the subdivision. I was actually throwing my legs up on clear glass. Slip-n-Slide took on new meaning with my revelation. I told Jeff, "If someone is driving home late at night, and his headlights hit our window at just the right moment, he is getting a full moon, regardless of the lunar phase!"

My friend Lane, who has a son with autism, said to me once during those long months, "I know all too well how it feels to be so out of control of something, but you can find great comfort in being with people who understand your frustration." I took Lane's advice and began talking in person and online with others fighting the fertility battle.

Certain bloggers and thread talkers blamed their miscarriages and inability to conceive on our shared clotting disorder, MTHFR. They applied a vulgar curse word label that mimics its initials. Many of the irritated, frustrated online community members dubbed the lucky women who easily conceived as "fertiles." I did feel less lonely, but as I continued to research my condition and read the other women's stories, I began to solemnly realize I may never conceive. But as a mother I perfectly understood my goal: *a baby*. God had even more in mind.

This Ain't Your Grandmama's Adoption

*Who would ever think that so much went on
in the soul of a young girl?
We all live with the objective of being happy;
our lives are all different and yet the same.*

—Anne Frank, *The Diary of Anne Frank*

Jeff and I had never *not* considered adoption. My sweet husband was adopted in 1963, when he was ten weeks old. We simply (ignorantly) thought infant adoptions were a thing of the past.

Jeff's was a typical agency adoption of those days. His birthmother was single, in college, and ashamed. According to our tiny stash of placement paperwork, written by a social worker, Jeff's birthmother "never waivered in her decision" to place him up for adoption. Jeff's birthparents relinquished their rights, and a foster mother took care of Jeff. While writing this book, I asked Jeff's mother to clarify for me what she experienced with infertility and Jeff's adoption almost a half-century ago.

She wrote the following:

Daddy Jeff and I started trying to have a baby after our first year of marriage. We tried for several years. I did not know anyone else who was having trouble getting pregnant. I had a lot of friends having babies, and it was difficult for me to hear them talk about their children because I wanted one so badly and I just kept starting my period.

Those days people did not talk about these kinds of issues like we do today, so I don't remember anyone saying strange things to me, but my doctor did a strange thing, I think!

My uterus was tilted so he put a block under it believing that might help me conceive. I never got to see if it would help because the next morning I couldn't use the bathroom!!! I had to rush back over to his office so he could remove the "block" because it stopped my ability to urinate. Looking back I think that was CRAZY. He tested Daddy Jeff, too. Those were our fertility treatment options in that period of time.

We lived in Nashville. Our social worker worked for the State of Tennessee. We had to fill out papers and answer all kinds of questions about what kind of child we wanted. Before the state would approve us, I had to quit my job and stay home for six months. I think they wanted women to be sure they were okay being homemakers. Back in those days, once you had a baby you didn't work. So, I quit my job in October, 1962 and was a homemaker for six months to prove I was ready to be a mother. We were approved in March, 1963. Then it was just a matter of waiting.

My sister Madolyn had a friend who owned a furniture business. We ordered a crib and a chest. We told the furniture maker we may not need the crib and chest for a long time; we would call him and have him drop ship the furniture when we got a baby. I bought nothing else because the social worker told us we may have a long wait ahead of us. But just four months later, on Friday, July 26, our social worker called us and said, "I have a baby for you."

The plan was for us to go to her office on Monday to discuss the baby boy's background and health history, go home Monday night and think things over, meet the baby on Tuesday, go home Tuesday night to think about whether or not we wanted that particular baby, and pick him up on Wednesday if we wanted to adopt him. I cried all day Saturday.

I was terrified, excited, and worried because I really didn't know if I was going to be a good mom.

We called Madolyn's friend and asked him to ship the bed and dresser. Daddy Jeff and I went shopping. We bought diapers—back then they were cloth—diaper pins, rubber pants, and pajamas. We called all our family and friends and told them the big news.

I remember sitting at the social worker's desk on Monday. Our social worker explained that the baby was born May 13, 1963. His birthmother was in college and his birthfather was a semi-professional. I wondered "Semi-professional what?" but I didn't ask. You just didn't ask those types of questions those days.

Our social worker explained that the birthmother denied her pregnancy until close to delivery because she didn't want to tell her parents. She was ashamed. Also, she and the birthfather had religious differences.

Both of the birthparents' rights were already terminated.

The social worker told us the baby may have red hair and asked if that would bother us.

I told her, "Absolutely not. We have red hair in our family, too."

She asked if it was okay if the baby was athletic and if we would support him if he wanted to play sports. Again, I answered, "Absolutely." She also told us the baby had a heart murmur, which is why the doctor required him to stay in foster care until he was ten weeks old. Back then, typically, adoptive parents got their babies at six weeks old.

Our social worker told us to go home, think about all we'd learned, and come back Tuesday at 11:00 a.m. to meet the baby. I pleaded with her (with my mind already made up) to let us take him home Tuesday, if possible, because Jeff had to go to Virginia for two weeks to attend his graduation from The Virginia School of Banking. She said she'd see what she could do. So, when we went back on Tuesday, hoping we would bring our baby home that afternoon, we took a little blue outfit, the one you have, Jody, and all the other things baby Jeff would need. Daddy Jeff wore a suit and tie and I wore a pleated Paquette skirt, hose, and high heels.

When we got to the social worker's building, we talked in her downstairs office and then she took us upstairs to a little nursery room. There wasn't much in there, just a little baby bed. Daddy Jeff and I walked over to the baby bed and looked in. Jeff was wearing a pale yellow sleeveless cotton diaper shirt and matching rubber pants.

I still get chills when I remember that day and walking into the nursery.

When we looked at Jeff, he smiled up at us like he knew us, like he was saying, "Here I am."

Love at first sight.

To this day, I cannot think about that day or tell that story without crying. I remember that as soon as we looked into the baby bed, the social worker left the room and quietly closed the door behind her. I picked Jeff up first. We held him for I don't know how long, before the social worker came back in the nursery room. She asked us if we wanted to adopt him. We said, "YES! YES! YES! We want to take him home!"

She had worked things out with the agency so that we could leave for two hours, not overnight, and come back to get Jeff. She told us to consider if he reminded us of someone we did not like, were we really ready to go through with an adoption. I didn't care about that but I guess some people did. They always wanted you to leave and think.

We drove close by to Baptist Hospital. The hospital had a drugstore with a soda fountain. That was our version of fast food back then. We sat in a booth next to a window and literally counted the minutes— one hundred and twenty—until we could go back and get Jeff. That was the longest lunch of our lives. When we returned to the social worker's office, we changed Jeff's diaper and put him in the little blue suit. He just smiled the whole time; he was so sweet. Of course, I held Jeff in my lap all the way home. My mother and daddy, and Jeff's brother Dillard, his wife Marie, and their six-month old Keith were waiting for us on the carport. From then until 10:00 p.m., sixty-eight people came to meet baby Jeff. My daddy was so proud, he shuttled back and forth to work I don't know how many times, bringing different groups of friends to see his grandson.

Daddy Jeff left on Saturday to go to Virginia and I was terrified. I was scared to go to sleep, in case baby Jeff needed me.

I watched him all day and all night. I lost eight pounds in the two weeks Daddy Jeff was gone.

Our company continued to visit. The front door was a revolving door. Our families and friends were so happy and excited.

The only negative thing anyone said actually came when I took Jeff for his first visit to our pediatrician. We discussed Jeff's heart murmur and the doctor said, "You know, you don't have to keep this baby."

I said, "Oh, yes I do!"

The adoption process was much simpler and much less expensive back then. Remember, abortions were illegal in the United States in 1963, so there were many more babies available for adoption.

The fertility treatment and adoption industries are dynamic; both change and evolve from year to year. Medical innovation and societal changes consistently, dramatically impact the baby business.

Just as Jeff's parents' fertility problems were treated differently in 1963, so was Jeff's adoption.

In 1963, fertility treatments were extremely limited. Now women may carry two embryos from different families and have twins who are not biologically related.

Jeff is almost an antique himself at forty-nine years old. As an infant Jeff enjoyed sweet Caro corn syrup in his bottle. Babies born today drink organic soy milk and engineered formula. When Jeff's parents brought him home from the foster home to meet family and friends, to keep six-month-old Keith occupied and out of the way, Keith's parents put him in a walker on tall wheels and used a long rope to tie his walker to a pole in the carport. Today, if a walker shows any signs of hazardous flaws, the manufacturer recalls the entire production line.

Jeff and I frequently discussed adoption but all the families we knew who had adopted had done so a decade or more before.

Plus, we assumed it was financially out of reach. We thought simple, in-state, inexpensive adoptions like Jeff's were now as scarce as cloth diapers and drug store soda fountains.

I did not see many positive stories in the news or movies about Americans adopting American babies. If I did, they were usually tumultuous stories full of betrayal, or tricks, or fear. I figured I would have to travel to China, or Russia, to get a baby. I ordered brochures from international adoption agencies, but once I saw the fee schedules, my optimism faded. By this time I had been trying to conceive for close to six years.

Then I saw the movie *Juno,* which came out in 2007. The movie truly opened my eyes. I was a chunky, Appalachian American, middle-class version of Jennifer Garner's character. After seeing *Juno* and the American public's reaction to it, I realized domestic adoption must be more common than I knew even though the adoptive couple in the movie was wealthy. I decided to do a little research.

How Does Will Turn To Way?

Some people go to priests; others to poetry;
I to my friends.

—Virginia Woolf, *The Waves*

In February 2008 I called my friend Kiki, who adopted her son and daughter in 1991 and 1996, respectively. I told her Jeff and I were considering adoption, but we did not know if there were any babies out there, if we could afford the process, or where to start. Kiki was the first to explain that domestic adoption can be affordable. She mailed me a stack of agency brochures, state and private agency contact numbers, an old newspaper article about her family, and a personal note that read:

> *Jody, Most of this info is over ten years old, but it may help. You never know...the more eggs you put in your adoption basket, the more likely one is to hatch! Above all else...PRAY!*

With this gentle boost from Kiki, I began an adoption investigation.

I called Kiki's list of agencies, crisis pregnancy centers, the Department of Child Services, and roamed the Internet. When I called Bethany Christian Services, an angel named Mark Akers answered the phone. Mark Akers is a "domestic adoption specialist" social worker. He answered my rapid-fire questions with empathy, respect, and patience, and he invited me to Bethany's monthly information meeting. Jeff and Houston had basketball practice, so I took my mother.

That same week I went to my last appointment with my fertility specialist.

Jeff and I drove to the doctor's office, anticipating a lengthy conversation about my pregnancy prognosis and future options. We had been seeing him for years and had a good relationship with him.

I really had only one important question: "Am I a healthy candidate for in-vitro?" I secretly wanted him to say, "No," so I could proceed without doubt toward adoption.

When I signed in at the front desk, the receptionist asked me to complete a new form. I took the clipboard and pen and sat beside Jeff, in a stiff chair against the wall. I looked down to see "Debit Card Agreement." The legalese basically stated that, at any time, the doctor could draft our checking account for any unpaid fees. I had been going there for years. We had spent my retirement fund on unsuccessful fertility treatments. I knew I still owed him about $1800, but I had also paid him thousands, and I was paying every month. That had never been a problem. It was so strange. I petitioned the front office nurse to allow me talk to my doctor. She said, "Let me go ask him." When she rather quickly returned to the waiting room, she said, "If you don't sign the debit card agreement, he won't see you." Jeff and I could not afford to sign that form.

One of the problems with fertility treatments is that you have to do them while you are young and your eggs are healthy. You cannot postpone treatments until you save all of the necessary money. By then, your eggs will be cracked!

I sobbed the whole time I was there and all the way home, more from humiliation and emotional fatigue than disappointment. All the way down Northshore Drive toward Glen Cove, Jeff cursed the doctor and his staff. Like Tom Wingo in *The Prince of Tides*, I "shut down like a broken motor." Once home, I slumped into our bed. I wallowed and wailed in defeat, confusion, embarrassment, and annoyance for some time. Jeff came into the bedroom to check on me and stated, "No more fertility stuff. We are getting our baby through adoption." With renewed hope, I wrote to Baby #2 on March 22, 2008.

> *Dear Baby,*
>
> *I had two big appointments this week. Daddy and I went to the fertility doctor's office where we were turned away because we would not sign over our bank account for drafts. Well, who can do that? I took Grandmama with me to Bethany Christian Services where we learned about domestic adoption, USA babies! When we left the meeting, Grandmama and I felt informed and giddy. I know you are on your way, somehow... and it may take a little more heartache, time, and effort on my part. We are going through Bethany to try to adopt you. Maybe God is letting me suffer so I will be able to empathize with your birthmother. I began praying for her last night. We have to get some financial things straightened out, but we plan to submit our preliminary application on April 15, 2008, our ninth wedding anniversary! See you soon?*
> *Love,*
> *Mama*

I wrote in Baby #2's journal that Jeff and I had to get "financial things straightened out" because, at the onset, we were in no *cash* position to begin the adoption process. I was new to the complex world of adoption, but I estimated that our total cost could range from ten to twenty thousand dollars. We did not have it, but I remembered someone telling me once, "If what you are doing is right with God, the money will show up."

I was also inspired to begin such an undertaking with no money by my cousin Sallie. Sallie is creative, brilliant, and strong-willed. Years into her impressive career in a large corporation, senior management officials called her into a special meeting. They praised her contributions, insight, and natural leadership abilities. They promised her she was on the fast track to executive success and could likely be president of that region at a very young age. Sallie resigned the next day. When I asked her why, she said, "I just thought about spending every day there the rest of my working life and it sounded so depressing." Sallie went to work, for minimum wage, for a suicide prevention hotline, and she loved it.

I know a few adoptive parents who saved for years to be financially ready. I admire their work ethic, and I wish I were a better saver, but I think that thought process is akin to the cliché "we can't afford to have a baby right now." I determined that a secular concept like money would not get in the way of my spiritual mission! With her stellar credit rating and eagerness to welcome another grandchild, my mother set up a line of credit at her bank to ensure we would not miss a baby opportunity due to lack of funds. I also did some creative financing (more on that later).

Look Anywhere for Inspiration

Storms make trees take deeper roots.

—Dolly Parton

With that entry, I began using the Baby #2 journal as a therapeutic outlet as well as a way to document our child's adoption story. I wanted at least nine months worth of anticipatory journaling so my potential adopted child and Houston would be "even" from the start. I also thought any recorded information would help my adopted child feel grounded, anticipated, and loved. The adoption journey is fascinating and eventful and what child would not want to read about the creative way in which he or she entered the world?

A huge source of inspiration and therapy came from an unlikely venue. MTV premiered its hit series, "16 and Pregnant." The show documented real life teenagers throughout their crisis pregnancies. I could not stomach the show's first five episodes. I held deep resentment toward any teenager who became pregnant. I felt the show's stars had no business being parents while I had every right to be. So, I did not watch until I caught a trailer for Episode Six.

That episode would feature Catelynn and Tyler, who were considering adoption for their unborn daughter. MTV gave no hint as to how Catelynn and Tyler's story would end. I wrote the date down in my planner.

On July 16, 2009, the night the episode aired, I banned Houston and Jeff from the living room. I proactively used the bathroom and fixed myself a glass of sweet tea. Then I dragged my rocking chair to face the television head-on. For an hour, I sat and watched, in awe and fear, as Catelynn and Tyler's story slowly unfolded. I did not budge during commercial breaks, for fear I would miss one word.

A few minutes into the program, cameras followed Catelynn and Tyler as they walked into a brick building. When a graphic appeared at the bottom of the screen reading "Bethany Christian Services Adoption Agency," I lost my breath. I had no clue they were using the same agency Jeff and I were. Four people existed in the universe in that moment, even though millions watched. Catelynn, Tyler, Dawn (the Bethany social worker), and I worked through the particulars of adoption before we met potential parents Brandon and Theresa. Once they appeared, I was miserable. I cried and willed my way through to the end of the episode, really struggling when Catelynn and Tyler kept lingering with baby Carly as Brandon and Teresa, powerless, waited down the hall. I felt so sorry for them (for me).

Finally, praise God, Brandon and Teresa met Carly in Catelynn's hospital room. I was mesmerized and enlightened by the birthparents' loving attitude toward the adoptive parents, and vice versa. Catelynn was the first birthmother I "met." Juno helped me, but Catelynn was real. I thought to myself, *Maybe a birthmother somewhere is watching Catelynn and Tyler. Maybe this show will help me get a baby.*

Grief and Grief in Reverse

A pity beyond all telling is hid in the heart of love.

—William Butler Yeats, "The Pity of Love"

Several of my friends underwent fertility treatments to have healthy and successful pregnancies. I am not, in any way, condemning fertility treatments, doctors, or patients. In my case infertility treatments took a negative toll on my spirit, marriage, body, finances, and attitude toward others. In retrospect I am still sad, yet thankful, that my treatments did not work.

Adopting a baby does not cure the lost opportunity of a biological child. I dreamed of a daughter, in fact, and probably would have had up to four boys to get her. When we applied at Bethany Christian Services, we asked for a girl. I would name my daughter Hattie-Scott after my childhood neighbor, Hattie Elder and my late father, Scott Cantrell. Hattie was eighty years old when I met her. Our house was at the dead end of a holler and Mrs. Elder lived at the beginning. My cousins and I often rode our bicycles down the gravel road to see our intriguing neighbor. After her baths, she sat on the top step of her farmhouse porch and combed her long gray hair, then spun it into a tight bun secured with bobby pins. She always wore sweatpants, a camisole, a blouse, an apron, and beaded necklaces. She entertained us with terrible tea and hard candy that required delicate extraction from a sticky cluster else we would shatter the glass biscuit jar container. Best of all, she was a story teller. She said things like, "If it don't touch the bottom of the pot, it don't taste right"—meaning all food tastes better fried in butter in a skillet.

To this day, she fascinates me. I dreamed of dressing my daughter in old-timey fabrics. I would pass down my mud-pie baking secrets: I swiped real eggs from the kitchen and took sugar packets from restaurants to make mud pies when I was little. I dreamed of enjoying an intimate, life-long, mother-daughter relationship, like the one I enjoy with my mother.

In October of 2009, I took Houston to the Tennessee Fall Homecoming festival at the Museum of Appalachia in Clinton, Tennessee. He listened to fiddlers and dulcimer players and watched harnessed mules slowly plod in a circle to press sugar cane for molasses making. I bought tiny handmade sunbonnets for my someday daughter to wear. No matter where I was or what I was doing, I was always thinking about my next child, and I was determined to have my way—my daughter, Hattie.

If you have chosen adoption, do not feel guilty about still wanting a biological child. After stopping fertility treatments I felt a huge sense of relief while also entering a period of grief. I said goodbye to the expectation that I would deliver my own child and hello to an alternative route.

In other words, I left "being processed" and entered "the process."

The Guided Tour through Hell to Heaven

My passions were all gathered together
like fingers that made a fist.
Drive is considered aggression today,
I knew it then as purpose.

—Bette Davis, *The Lonely Life*

When our social worker, Mark, first asked me why I was pursuing adoption, I replied, "I am tired of wearing a lab coat to bed."

Mark is a devout Christian; I dedicated this book to him because he is the most sincere and consistent witness to the lessons of Jesus Christ I have ever known. But he needed to learn right off the bat that I am not a Bible-thumping do-gooder, nor did I ever feel "called" to adopt. I had a broken spirit and a desperate desire for another child. Mark has a great sense of humor and helps hopeful parents from all walks of life with all kinds of reasons for seeking a child through adoption. Mark was the perfect guide for me. He is also his daughter's softball coach and a big college football fan. He was the perfect social worker for Jeff.

When people who are debating domestic versus international versus state custody adoptions ask me why Jeff and I chose domestic, I tell them, "We weighed our risk tolerance, financial resources, time commitment, marital strength, and emotional and spiritual stamina against the requirements of each type of adoption. *You* have to choose the adoption that best matches *your* resources." Jeff and I chose domestic adoption because it was affordable and because we were better suited to negotiate with American birthparents than with a foreign government. Yes, American birthparents can change their minds after a baby's birth, and there are many legal risks, but if a foreign government lost my documents or political problems or corruption caused that country to suspend U.S. adoptions, Jeff and I would be toast, financially. Based on our high emotional and low financial risk-tolerances, Jeff and I deemed domestic adoption doable for us. For the first time in years, I felt optimistic.

On April 15, 2008, my ninth wedding anniversary, Houston and I visited Bethany Christian Services and I gave Mark our preliminary application.

Mark asked Houston, then six years old and in kindergarten, "Are you excited?"

Houston answered, "Yes, sir. So what do we do? Just come back in two weeks and get our baby?"

"Well, Houston, it takes a little bit longer than that," Mark explained. "Once your family is approved, you may wait anywhere from a few days to two years."

The very next day Houston announced to his elementary school principal, "Ms. Hill, I'm getting a baby when I'm eight years old!"

Houston

For-ev-ER... For-ev-ER... For-ev-ER!

—"Squints" in *The Sandlot*

Existing children of waiting parents must also lumber through the adoption obstacle course. Houston dealt with a mother who endured routine heartbreak via monthly negative pregnancy tests and whose moods swung like a heavy pendulum due to artificial hormones. I recall a time when I felt nauseated, and my period was late.

Houston, then about four years old, and I were in our backyard. I was watching him play with plastic soldiers in a little mud hole. We chatted about his ongoing miniature war between the Americans and Germans when I felt a familiar cramp-like sensation in my abdomen. I knew what it meant.

At that moment, my innocent and enthusiastic Houston said, "Mama, watch these Americans attack the bad guys! Mama, Mama, watch!"

My eyes were closed. My mental efforts were acutely zeroed in on my slight stomach cramp. I hatefully snapped, "Houston, leave me alone a minute!"

Poor Houston, an only child often in the middle, bounced between a mother overwrought, anxious, and sad, a father stressed out by his own sense of loss and frustration, and parents trying to manage fertility, then adoption, expenses.

Most importantly, Houston longed for a sibling. The adoption process is loaded with "maybes," but Houston talked about his future sibling in concrete terms. I often cautioned, "You know, Houston, we may never get a baby."

Tired of hearing my doubt, he began retorting, "I know! It's okay. Quit saying that! Ughhhh."

His level of understanding, enthusiasm, and engagement was often questioned by relatives and friends. Jeff and I informed Houston because it was an incredible opportunity for him to learn about family, delayed gratification, patience, open-mindedness, martial communication and commitment, decision-making, and prayer.

Helpful, Hurtful, and Ridiculous Reactions

Once we submitted the preliminary application, hoping for support and word-of-mouth advertising, we told friends and family we were "trying to adopt." Hey, that is the best advertising, right? I met Jeff on a blind date and heard about my first job from a friend, so why not tell folks to be on the lookout for a baby?

All of my friends were fired up: they professed certainty that I would soon have a baby in my arms. Other folks, even very close family members, expressed doubt. Some said nothing at all. I was surprised by the reactions I got, and I was surprised by who said what. Misinformed people quipped, "Oh, that's so nice of you to adopt. You are saving a child."

When I felt up to it, I gently explained, "This is as hard as hell and it would be much easier to be pregnant. I am not saving this baby. His birthmother will save him by not aborting him. She is saving me."

One of my favorites was when a good friend said, ignorantly but sweetly, "Wow, by the time you get this baby, you may think this was harder than being pregnant."

I responded, quite amused, "Yes, I do believe that eight years will be harder than nine months."

A question I despised was, "Is Jeff really on board with this adoption thing?"

That question was especially offensive because Jeff was adopted.

Plus, you may be able to trick your husband into a pregnancy, but there is no way to trick him into adopting. He has to trek through the gauntlet next to you every difficult step of the way.

A relative asked me, "Are you sure you should be telling Houston all this?"

On that one, I consulted Mark and Terri, the Knoxville Bethany office director, on whether or not it was a good idea to keep Houston so informed. They advised Jeff and me to tell Houston the good, the bad, and a limited version of the ugly so he would feel valued in the process. When most couples decide to have a second or third child, they do not consult their existing children. For some reason I had to convince people that Houston wanted a sibling.

Waiting adoptive parents should be tolerant and forgiving. Friends and family love you and want you to have a child, but they are not privy to the information you have and are relegated to arm chair quarterback positions.

Looking back, I think "doubters" were grappling with their own biases and worries, on our behalf. They did not want us, especially Houston, to suffer. But suffering is a pre-requisite to adopting.

Trust me, when your baby arrives, everyone you know will shower him or her with love and acceptance!

I've Got a Bite!

Not only so, but we also glory in our sufferings,
because we know that suffering produces
perseverance; perseverance, character;
and character, hope.

—Romans 5:3-4

My big-mouth advertising quickly paid off. Read this email I sent to friends on May 15, 2008, exactly one month after I submitted our preliminary application to Bethany.

Friends, I need you to pray for me. Through word-of-mouth from my cousin and a bank employee, I met a woman from Harriman, Tennessee Friday night over the phone who is pregnant with twin girls, due May 27! She has hired an adoption attorney and is looking for adoptive parents ASAP. The babies weigh 3 ½ and 4 ½ pounds and are healthy. I want to pursue this chance and meet with her but Jeff is afraid (two?). LOTS of things would have to fall in place, and we would have to agree on the adoption plan but I am hopeful.

I got this call on Jeff's birthday! It was Jeff's birthday seven years ago that I found out I was pregnant with Houston. My mother talked to me yesterday morning as she waited to go into school and as she was talking to me, identical twin boy students were making funny faces at her through the car window. I have to wonder about all these coincidences. Jeff's parents were wary of this opportunity, which reinforced Jeff's fears. I think he can handle two girls just fine, and I have the most to lose if he can't. Will you pray that God's will will be done? I am terrified that Jeff's fear is causing us to make the wrong decision and go against what God intends. Thank you.

Emails poured in offering support, giving suggestions, and adding to my confusion.

One of my oldest friends, Marilyn, wrote back.

Here is what Jeff should think about; what is the difference if you were to get pregnant with twins? Well, there you go, you now have 3 children. Maybe it's a little sooner than expected, but not really, when you think about how long you guys have waited for this.

A cousin questioned.

Maybe he's afraid that he'll say yes and something will happen like the mother changing her mind and that would be so very painful.

Joe, a friend-of a friend, offered help.

I know three couples who had great difficulty conceiving and now each have a set of twins.

Is two at a time a lot to take care of ...absolutely, but at the end of the day, no one has lost his mind, no one has gone bankrupt, no one has endured an appreciable hardship of any kind and ultimately those fleeting moments of frustration have been replaced with the blessed sound of children playing. None of them would exchange a moment of extra work of two for that extra child. Remember that sometimes when God opens up Heaven to let out a blessing, it doesn't just rain...it pours.

On Friday night, the birthmother told me, "I feel cautiously optimistic about you. Talk to your husband and call me back in a few days." I followed her instructions. When we spoke again, the birthmother said she did not intend to tell the birthfather about the babies. I explained that we could not consider taking them without the birthfather waiving his rights. She said she would think about it and call me back.

Distraught over Jeff's and my in-laws' reactions and the suspense and stress surrounding these two baby girls, I drove to a prayer path at the Presbyterian church down the street from my home. Houston accompanied me. We walked a pea-gravel lined labyrinth, built by a Boy Scout seeking Eagle status years ago. In the center of the labyrinth, Houston witnessed me release a deluge of tears and commentary and prayer. I asked Houston to pray for us. He bowed his freckled face and whispered, "God, please give my mama two babies in a row."

People who are waiting for a baby toggle between prayerful, hopeful rest in the calm eye—the wait—and nerve-wracking clashes with the eye wall—the mental work of adoption. With the Harriman twins, I faced ferocious winds of panic from Jeff and his parents. I faced winds of legal problems regarding the birthfather. I faced winds of financial stress that would inevitably come with a private (non-agency) adoption and with raising twin girls.

God made his plan perfectly clear or perhaps the birthmother's free will interrupted the plan. Either way, I never talked to the woman again.

I was distraught. I felt like all the "signs" were there, but when I tried to call her, she did not answer. I even left messages with the bank employee in Harriman who knew the birthmother; she never called me back. That beautiful opportunity to bring home and raise two daughters appeared out of nowhere, and then vanished in what felt like a split second. Jeff, Houston, and I encountered a varied range of surprising emotions and attitudes. I felt like a fool. The experience beat me down, back into the wistful eye, and there was where I regained strength and hope.

Wait for the LORD;
Be strong and let your heart take courage;
Yes, wait for the LORD.

—Psalm 27:14

Understated Cliché:
Adoption Is a Roller Coaster Ride

The beauty of the world, which is so soon to perish,
has two edges, one of laughter, one of anguish,
cutting the heart asunder.

—Virginia Woolf, *A Room of One's Own*

Growing up in Sevier County, Tennessee, "The Gateway to the Great Smoky Mountains," my cousins and I spent summer days at Dolly Parton's theme park Dollywood gobbling funnel cakes, clogging to "Rocky Top" and "Barefootin'" (songs sung by our own relatives in a Dollywood amphitheatre) and riding rides. The adoption journey is often compared to a roller coaster ride. I think it is more like Dollywood's Log Flume.

At first, Jeff and I waited with hundreds of others in a long line, speculating on the future. Then we clumsily boarded the little log boat and got uncomfortably close to each other and to strangers. Our boat lurched out of the boarding dock.

We relinquished control and safety to people we did not know. For snatches of time, we cruised. Now and then the channel narrowed, and our little boat jerked and knocked against walls. We looked outside the ride to see dry, happy, carefree vacationers, and we thought, *Why did we get on this uncomfortable ride? How will we look when we get off this boat?* We methodically ascended to a peak with no visible next course. From the top, for a second, we enjoyed a privileged treetop view of the beautiful park and Smokies beyond. In an instant, we furiously plunged into ice cold water. Soaked, we slid into the dock, hoping the mid-descent photo was not hideous and that we did not drop all of our money on the ride.

With the Harriman twins we endured all of that except we did not spend any money. Next, we got back in line to ride again.

So Personal and So Public

*I'm extraordinarily patient
provided I get my own way in the end.*

—Margaret Thatcher

The adoption process involved pretty much everyone we knew. It is disheartening to think that a decision like having a baby that is usually so private has to be so public. Adoption should be a lovely, wonder-filled, positive journey of Godly inspiration and happy experiences, right?

As Mark Akers warns, it is sometimes a "raw experience." I once heard another adoptive mother say that when she and her husband decided to pursue adoption, they invited both sides of the family to brunch to discuss the decision. I laughingly commented, "Just think, if you and your husband decided to have sex in hopes of conceiving, no one else would be involved! You certainly would not host a brunch to talk about it!"

Adoption is an industry and waiting parents cannot be wimps. There are layers and layers of paperwork.

My friend Laura, who was waiting for her son from Ethiopia when we met, often wore a t-shirt that read, "No morning sickness but the paper cuts are killing me."

At one point, I had an eighty-two-item to-do list. Agencies' requirements vary. Bethany required tax returns, financial statements, written recommendations from our pastor, family members, and close friends, medical check-ups for Jeff, Houston, and me, shot records for our Yorkie, Buzz, drug tests, finger prints, and so on. Bethany also required us to do extensive soul-searching on paper. I have taken plenty of tests, but these were the toughest questions I had ever answered. Jeff and I each completed a 51-question self-study with prompts like the following:

- *Briefly explain the events in your life that you feel have shaped your personality.*
- *How has your marriage changed since the honeymoon?*
- *Describe a problem in your marriage; explain how you worked it out.*
- *What are your relationships with each other's families?*
- *How will you promote the values and character you want to develop in your children?*
- *How would you feel if your child decides to search for his/her birthparents?*

One of my favorites was "What role does your physical relationship play in your marriage?" On this one, Jeff answered, "An important one."

I felt tremendous, self-inflicted pressure to adequately communicate who we were in a positive light on paper. So much was at stake.

We told the truth about who we really are, and answered the questions in a conversational manner, taking topics seriously but revealing our personalities. Jeff, the habitual procrastinator, was never much of a student and those questions, along with a required written statement of faith, proved daunting for him.

Big Chick If You Have To

My Great Aunt Betty had an admirable ability to make her husband and children do what was right. Once, her husband Bill was unemployed for a time. She became fed up and tricked him into getting into their car. She drove to Luken Chevrolet in LaGrange, Georgia, and ordered, "You have been sitting at home long enough. Get out of the car. Go in there and talk to that manager. I will sit right here and wait. Don't come back to this car without a job!"

A while later, Uncle Bill came back to the car and said, "He told me to start at 9:00 a.m. tomorrow."

Betty also busted up a relationship of which she did not approve between her son and a girlfriend. To help her grown daughter finish college, Betty, a grandmother, enrolled herself in the same school and made straight A's. She sported bottle-blonde curly permed hair, and after she established this pattern of rule, her children deemed her "Big Chick."

Big Chick began as a proper noun and ended as a verb. I had to "Big Chick" Jeff to get his self-study and statement of faith completed.

Jeff admits he has a procrastination problem. In his self-study, to the question "Describe your personality," Jeff answered, "I am patient and don't get mad often. It's important to have a positive attitude. My weakness is that I always think nothing can go wrong and I can be a procrastinator."

One night, fed up with Jeff's foot-dragging, I pinned him down with wifely threats. He plopped into a club chair in our den. I sat across from him at the computer and directed, "I'm going to ask these questions. You answer, I'll type, and we'll finally be through with your paperwork."

A few questions in, I congratulated myself thinking, *This is working!* But, ten minutes later, Jeff started slurring his very important words and rubber necking. He slid down the chair like Tom the Cat down a staircase after being conked on the head by Jerry's bat.

I asked, "What is wrong with you?"

"I didn't sleep well last night so I took one of your mother's tranquilizers."

Furious, I refused to let him off the hook. I woke him up question by question (yes, I yelled). He answered. We finished. Jeff's answers were brief, sincere, and, finally, on paper. Yippee!

Please know that if infertility stress does not cause a few knock-down-drag-out fights, the adoption process will. Your marriage is not falling apart: it is being tested and growing stronger. Plus, you may learn a thing or two. I like to joke that Jeff's documents required stapled addendums and "please explain here" lines. That drunken thirtieth birthday party when you smarted off to a policeman and landed in the clinker wearing only a wet swimsuit may come back to haunt you fifteen years later!

I am not bashing Jeff. Parents who are just beginning the process need to understand that perfection is neither expected nor required. Be yourself. Tell the truth. Embrace the process.

Despite my marital harassment and Jeff's procrastination, Jeff's answers were unspoiled, genuine, and charming. Shakespeare writes, "Brevity is the soul of wit." Asked how Jeff and I are different, Jeff wrote, "Jody is country and I am city."

To the question "What does freedom in a marriage mean to you?" Jeff replied, "Doing stuff you want to do but doing things the right way."

When prompted "Describe your child," I penned a colorful, verbose description of all things Houston. Jeff simply wrote, "Houston is a mini Jeff Dyer." Enough said!

Beggars Must Choose

There are no such things as limits to growth,
because there are no limits to the human capacity
for intelligence, imagination, and wonder.

—Ronald Reagan

The most challenging document we completed was the "Openness Options" questionnaire. It is a *yes/no/will consider* checklist of tormenting decision points. Remember that you really cannot predict exactly what your "situation" will look like.

Mark counseled that, right or wrong, most adoptive parents can not say no to a baby once they meet one. The openness questionnaire helps social workers match adoptive parents to birthparents, and the questionnaire helps both parties make calm, informed decisions before a baby arrives. These are points any adoptive couple should consider, whether they are using an agency, a lawyer, foster care, or word-of-mouth advertising to find a child.

Here is a brief list of some of the many decision points in our multi-page questionnaire:

Birth family Involvement
- Meet birthparents and their families
- Hospital contact (our presence at delivery)
- Birthparent participation in naming of child
- Legal risk placement: direct placement in the home from the hospital before parental rights are terminated
- Visitation after placement (how often, how long, level of communication)

Medical History
- Limited information, no information
- Baby is product of rape, date rape, incest
- Mental illness in birth family
- Drug/alcohol use – birthparents
- Criminality
- STDs, HIV
- No consistent prenatal care (or none at all)

Child
- Age
- Twins/multiples
- Permanent medical condition
- Race/Ethnicity/Nationality

I kept thinking, *Beggars can't be choosers*. Thank goodness for Mark. His guidance helped us check the right boxes for our family and steer clear of unnecessary guilt.

As we mulled over these possibilities, we kept in mind that when Jeff was adopted all his parents received was a two-page typed letter from a Child Welfare Trainee.

The letter briefly outlined Jeff's birthparents' height, weight, hair-color, and education level. His birthmother had no prenatal care. The only specific future-relevant fact written was "The natural father was athletically inclined and excelled in sports." Jeff clings to that short sentence.

Also, funny enough, Jeff's parents got that letter *after* they brought Jeff home.

Jeff and I chose what risks we could handle. We talked, prayed, stretched, and went for broke, especially on the legal risk placement questions.

It is possible for a birthparent to call off the adoption at the child's birth: several women I know have left the hospital with empty car seats and shattered dreams. Some have even taken the baby home, cared for him or her for days, weeks, or months, praying the birthparents would relinquish their rights, only to have one or both birthparents change attitudes and ask for the baby back.

Laws regarding the timing of child placement with adoptive parents and the termination of rights of birth parents vary from state to state. Jeff and I put Houston and ourselves in a potentially heartbreaking situation because we wanted birthparents to know we were fully invested and because we wanted our baby to know we anticipated our baby's birth with confidence and joy.

Our most important piece of paperwork was the "Dear Birthparent" letter. Jeff and I were tasked with summarizing who we are as a family on one typed page that would be our first communication with birthparents. The letter went in the front of our family profile (a photo booklet depicting our family, friends, home, and lifestyle) and on the Bethany website for prospective birthparents to see—nationwide!

How do you articulate who you are, explain what a child's life will be like in your home, and set yourself apart from thousands of other waiting parents? How do you communicate with an unknown person who may give you her child?

Jeff began his letter, "I feel like I have something in common with your child. I am adopted myself and understand how it feels to be loved by an adoptive mother and father…I think about my birthparents and how blessed I am that they were strong enough to choose adoption for me…I hope that somebody will give me the opportunity to give a child the same love and commitment."

I began my letter by bluntly writing, "Our promise to you: Jeff and I will always tell this child that you are a good, brave unselfish parent. We will make sure this precious child understands the immense depth of your sacrifice and love."

Houston also contributed to the letter. He said to me as I was working on our profile, "Why can't I write something in there?" I agreed to let him "in" on the letter. Houston said demonstratively, "Okay, type exactly what I say. Do not change anything!"

Houston's paragraph reads, "I hope we get the baby. I would love to see you. I will carry the baby around in a stroller in the grocery store. I will teach the baby how to swim. I think making the baby go to sleep will be the hardest thing. I would help the baby make friends. I will teach the baby how to read. I will jump around and make the baby laugh."

Even the Fun Stuff Isn't Easy

A line will take us hours maybe;
Yet if it does not seem a moment's thought,
our stitching and unstinting has been naught.

—William Butler Yeats, *Responsibilities*

The last piece of the paperwork puzzle to complete was the family profile book. I admit I felt competitive, which was ridiculous because adoptive families are as unique as the birthparents who choose them. I wanted our profile book to stand out from the stacks, communicate the child's future, and, like the "Dear Birthparent" letter, show an accurate, positive summary of life with the Dyers. I saved the profile book for last because I thought it would be fun and simple to assemble. I was wrong.

First, we did not have many family pictures of all three of us. I guess I was always behind the camera. Second, a variety of L'Oreal Preference shades caused my hair to change colors throughout the book. My mother, a University of Georgia journalism major, told me to make sure people's faces were at least as big as quarters.

I had a problem finding pictures of good times (beach trips, UT tailgates) without margaritas, wine glasses, or Michelob Ultra cans in sight. I did control the weather, though. The sun *always* shines and flowers constantly bloom in the Dyer yard! Oh, and the floors are spotless.

We needed a family photo of Houston, Jeff, and me to accompany our "Dear Birthparent" letter on the Bethany Christian Services national website and to serve as the cover photo for our family profile. The picture, to me, was crucial, as it would give a first impression to a national audience of birthparents on the Internet and sit in the local Bethany office for potential birthparents' viewing. At the corner of our front deck, our American flag hung just above three full-blooming Endless Summer hydrangeas. The blue sky, the pink blooms, and the American flag were a flawless backdrop for our family picture. We would look "hot dogs and apple pie." Confident in my plan, I called my dear neighbor Allyn and asked if she would please come take our picture.

Allyn is the dream neighbor for any child. She offers a swimming pool, wears beautiful bright clothes, cooks gourmet food (because of her, Houston loves Brie), and exudes originality and personality. To Houston's routine delight, she gets seemingly daily deliveries from United Parcel Service. The big truck parks at the bottom of her steep hill and Houston observes intently from his ESPN-watching perch in our living room as the men in brown tote parcels up the yard to her front door. "Allyn's getting another package," he will announce.

When I called Allyn to ask her to photograph us, she said, "Absolutely, but you guys will have to come over here because I have on my bathing suit." Now, I may seem petty here, but I will tell this story to highlight how often even the smallest tasks in the adoption process are sometimes frustrating and tricky. Jeff, Houston, and I, dressed in blue golf shirts and a pink blouse to match my hydrangeas, tromped up Allyn's hill for our photo session.

Wrapped in a beach towel and sipping something tropical, Allyn greeted us enthusiastically, saying "You all look beautiful! I want to take your picture in front of my flowers first." Allyn and I love to plant flowers and one summer we counted each other's flowerpots to see who was more out of control. Allyn won (or lost) fifty-one pots to my forty-nine. We posed behind her pool in front of dozens of herbs and flowers. Then Allyn got inspired.

"Oooh! I just got this new artsy lizard in the mail and hung it above my bench. That would be a cute picture," Allyn suggested. I did not have the heart to object, so the three Dyers sat on a mosaic tile bench under a wall-mounted reptile and smiled for the camera. Allyn remarked, "Yay! I got the whole lizard in that one."

When I downloaded the pictures, the bench photo was the best, except that the lizard's tale was pointed serpent-like right at my head. Also, we were flanked by a hand-painted fly swatter and a shelf full of Off bug spray. I cropped the picture. It was simple and perfect. Houston's face looked angelic.

In designing the profile book, I tried to consider what I would want to see if I were a birthmother. I wrote very little and put big, happy pictures of our home, our family, our friends, and holidays. I spent many mornings while Houston was at school, at the local Fed-Ex copy center sorting and cropping my way to a baby. I befriended Richard, a gregarious Fed-Ex employee who, visit after visit, guided me through equipment to save me a small fortune in copy fees. He helped me perfect our profile.

After our final printing, Richard proudly showed our finished mini-magazine to an intrigued crowd of Fed-Ex customers and demanded, "Who the hell wouldn't give this poor lady a baby?"

I Am Not Crazy. Neither Are You.

Every time I visited the Fed-Ex store to craft our profile book, I slid into the Expectant Mother Parking spot, boldly locking eyes with the flat metal teddy bear ornamenting a cutesy little sign at the front of the parking place. With my 80's-child attitude, I thought, *Gag me with a dead Smurf. I am freaking parking here.* I also parked in these sappy spaces at Target. *In your faces, "fertiles!"* I'd say to myself. I guess I was trying to convince myself that I was like any other pregnant woman.

Read this definition of pregnant from the *The Free Dictionary by Farlex* and tell me it does not, for the most part, describe someone waiting for a baby.

> **preg·nant**
> *adj.*
> **1.** Carrying developing offspring within the body.
> **2. a.** Weighty or significant; full of meaning.
> **b.** Of great or potentially great import, implication, or moment
> **3.** Filled or fraught; replete
> **4.** Having a profusion of ideas; creative or inventive.
> **5.** Producing results; fruitful

My burden felt much more intense than nausea, much heavier than pregnancy weight gain.

Like I said before, I entertained resentment toward pregnant women. At least with adoption you do not get fat— unless you eat when stressed.

During my pregnancy with Houston, I packed on some poundage. My doctor cautioned me to slow it down. I asked her what to change and she replied, "Eat the peach, not the cobbler."

I retorted, "Listen, I am eating guilt-free for the first time in my life. I'm riding this train all the way into the station!"

I gained fifty-five pounds and was a content whopper. I am thankful I enjoyed my pregnancy. I also formed a few healthy and unhealthy habits as we traveled the rigorous course of adoption. Everything about the adoption process is hard except loving the child. Waiting mother, you are not crazy. You are coping.

Bite by bite, Jeff and I ate the small elephant of paperwork and made all the necessary appointments. Some parents complete the paperwork in a short time, but Jeff and I took about a year. The infertility treatments and clinical nature of our sex life had pervaded and dominated our daily family life. So, though it was difficult for my impatient spirit, we put Houston's school and sports and other opportunities first and did the adoption paperwork as time and money allowed. When a friend asked me, "What all do you have to do to get approved?" I laughed and said, "Everything imaginable! I am writing the essay of my life and the prize is a heck of a lot bigger than a $500 scholarship check from the Gatlinburg Rotary Club."

The Suffer Club

While Jeff and I worked toward completing our application packet, I attended Bethany's "Waiting Families" support group meetings. Mark hosts the monthly meeting to educate and counsel waiting families. Waiting parents in the room are at different stages in the adoption process and bring different stories with them. Some have suffered great losses. Some have been waiting a long time already. Some have endured failed placements. Some know about a baby and will be parents in a matter of days or weeks.

I call the group the "Suffer Club" because everyone in that room is pensive, under great stress, and praying for a child. Mark leads the meetings, and he wholeheartedly teaches, reassures, and guides waiting parents.

Jeff, nicknamed "Tall Child" by my adoring mother, was not too keen on going to the Suffer Club with me. He said, "That's not my type of thing." Luckily, he had a routine, ready-made alibi in Houston's flag football, baseball, and basketball practices (Jeff coached or helped coach each team), but when he could, he did go with me. The first time Jeff *did* attend a meeting, we arrived early and waited in the Bethany parking lot a few minutes. I explained that this meeting was like a support group and that everyone participates.

Tall Child declared, "I'm not saying anything. You do all the talking for us." Jeff sat obligingly in a folding chair, facing a circle of men and women in similar situations who were also very different from him.

Fear, anxiety, mystery, pain and prayer heavily draped that conference room. Mark would start each meeting with an icebreaker question to lighten the mood. At that meeting, Mark asked us to introduce ourselves and answer, "What is your favorite restaurant?"

Jeff whispered in my ear, "La Paz."

I whispered back, "If you want to say La Paz, say it."

He said, "No, you say it for me." He was embarrassed to participate in a support group but definitely wanted to give a shout out to his favorite restaurant!

So, at my turn, I said, "I'm Jody Dyer. I love the Pancake Pantry in Gatlinburg. This is my husband Jeff. He is quiet and his favorite restaurant is La Paz."

Mark said, "Welcome Jeff! It's great to see you here."

Jeff smiled and nodded. Later in the meeting, we discussed how to explain adoption to our future children. Jeff suddenly raised his hand. Mark called on him. Jeff completely opened up to the group and told them about his own adoption and how his mother did an exceptional job of telling him his story, always showing respect when speaking of Jeff's anonymous birthparents. I was proud of him.

Mr. and Mrs. Dyer, regarding attitudes toward birthparents, were progressive thinkers in 1963. Then and now, they personify unconditional love.

I rarely missed a meeting. Listening to and learning from Mark, the Bethany staff, and other waiting, wondering parents helped me feel less isolated, more prepared, and considerably reassured.

Often, as Mark began the group talk with a prayer, I sneakily squinted and scanned the circle of fellow "waiters" in folding chairs to identify missing participants: new parents.

Now and then, Mark informed us of a successful placement and we rejoiced in empathetic unison. One could almost see the relief in our body language at such announcements. Our group prayed for specific families, birthparents, and babies, often by name.

Mark once asked us to brainstorm for topic ideas for the next meeting. I offered, "I know! We all should gather here and, for two hours, you repeat, 'You are going to get a baby. You are going to get a baby.' That's what we all want to hear. I'll bring cookies!"

On one of my solemn days in late 2006, I was shopping at the mall when my mother called. My cousin Toby, mother to Dan and Grady and pregnant with her third child, had had her mid-term ultrasound that morning. My ecstatic mother said "Toby's having a little girl! Finally, we'll have a little girl in the family again."

I was sincerely happy for Toby, but I was living in an abyss of frustration. I walked to Baby Bundles and bought something pink for my new pink cousin-on-the-way, who would be named Rosalind. A few minutes later, my mother called and told me my Aunt Judy (Toby's mother) and Toby were so excited they were going shopping and were headed to the mall. I headed to the door. I could not risk bumping into them. One look at my wrung out dishrag of a face would reveal I had been crying.

While struggling to conceive, pregnancy news induced resentment and self-pity. When struggling through the adoption wait, placement news thrilled and energized me.

Another Bite

Every problem has a gift for you in its hands.

—Richard Bach

Social workers and adoptive moms often reminded me that I could get a baby from anywhere in America, from any imaginable source, at any time, so I never dismissed rumors of babies or potential situations. I wrote again in the baby's journal October 6, 2008.

Dear Baby,
I had an interesting day. I saw Kiki in the grocery store. She said she'd heard from a friend, a social worker for the elderly, about a baby boy, two months old, in a bad situation. His mother left him with her friend, abandoned him, really. The friend took him to the birthmother's mother. This baby's grandmother is old, poor, and unable to take care of him.
The social worker called Kiki and Kiki told her I may be interested.
I want a girl but this situation intrigues me. She gave me the details. Not good. No one can find the

birthmother. I can't take a baby whose birthparents haven't terminated rights. I could keep him for months or years and they could show up and take him back. Laws tend to protect birthparents, understandably, but when you are the adoptive parents, that is terrifying. We could rescue that child, but the law is in the way. He's in a terrible situation. I will not pursue this child. That sounds awful. I tell you this because someday you will learn that life has some ugliness to it. And, adoption is a situation of mutual "choosing" if that makes sense.

Even through the pain of infertility, I thank God for Houston, our supportive family, and the possibility of you. A few days ago, Houston (now 6 ½) became furious with me because he realized I had given away his baby bath tub. He said, "I wanted to save that for our baby!" I promised him he could pick out a new one for you. He is excited about you but can't comprehend the wait. We love you concretely, even though you are so elusive, so seemingly far away, so much a dream.
Love,
Mama

Back to Life, Back to Reality

It's life. You don't figure it out.
You just climb up on the beast and ride.

—Rebecca Wells, *Divine Secrets of the Ya-Ya Sisterhood*

Decisions in the adoption process are difficult, of course, but often confusing. The Harriman babies and Kiki's rumored baby were like shooting stars: magical, mysterious, then gone. Jeff and I excessively contemplated each adoption-related decision and tried to predict its effect on our destiny. Disillusioned and determined by another dead end, I focused on completing our adoption paperwork requirements, being a good mother and wife, and saving money to pay for our home study. Jeff wanted to pay for adoption expenses, but he prioritized appropriately. He worried about the mortgage bill, electricity bill, phone bill, groceries, car payments, etcetera, so *I* had to ensure we were on task with financing the adoption.

I hustled any way I could to scrounge up the cash. I signed up to be a substitute teacher at Houston's school and our church day care. I made $52 a day at the elementary school and $40 at the daycare. I also hoodwinked my husband.

Inspired by character Viviane in *Divine Secrets of the Ya-Ya Sisterhood*, when I bought groceries, I wrote the check for ten or twenty dollars over the bill, and kept the change in my Bible, as if those Holy pages could neutralize my dishonesty. When I paid for some part of the adoption paperwork (a Bethany fee, Fed-Ex charges, doctor bills, fingerprinting costs, etc.), I sneaked to my Bible, slid stolen dollars from the thin pages, and bought cashiers checks.

I took care of baby business.

During my blissful years as a housewife, reality hit and I could no longer sneak my way through bill paying. The economy and our bank accounts dropped into a recession. Jeff was a realtor, and I was a middle-management banker turned housewife. I still joke that signs of the recession abound in the problematic plumbing and peeling paint around our house. We needed a second income again, but all the Knoxville area banking jobs were either commission-only mortgage originator positions (almost as bad as being a realtor in the recession) or low-paying jobs where, once we paid for Houston's after-school and summer care, would bring us only to a break even point.

I knew I needed to go back to work, but I worried that doing so would jeopardize our adoption chances. My lucrative career in banking kept Houston and me apart for ten-hour days. I feared a birthmother would not choose me if I relied on year-round daycare, so I stayed frugal and stayed home until I had no choice.

In the fall of 2009, I faced reality and went back to school to become a teacher. Most of the women and many of the men in my family were or are educators, so I felt comfortable with the career choice and financial compromise. Basically, I was trading money for time.

I figured there was no point putting my life on hold and jeopardizing my family's financial well-being in hopes of getting a baby.

I gambled that a birthmother would prefer a teacher's family-friendly schedule over a bank vice-president's hectic calendar.

In August 2009, I began the first of eighteen course hours of the Post-Baccalaureate program at Lincoln Memorial University in Harrogate, Tennessee. Fortunately, LMU caters to working adults, so instead of taking a sixty-mile haul to the main campus, I drove only twenty miles to satellite classrooms for bi-weekly, four-hour classes. My friend Karen (mother to four young children) and I carpooled to cut down on gas and misery. I also had to knock out nine hours of prerequisites and did so at Pellissippi State Community College in Knoxville.

My generous in-laws paid my LMU tuition, but I dipped into my "Bible" fund to pay for books and registration fees. I actually rented a few books online and guiltily borrowed from the Knox County Library—overdue book fines were much cheaper than campus bookstore prices. I kept up my grocery store thievery and substituted at Houston's school and the church daycare as much as possible. In the throes of the adoption process, I had initiated an arduous, inconvenient, expensive, lengthy two-year educational project and my master plan was way out of whack, but I remained focused on my goal: baby.

Par for the Course

Piglet sidled up to Pooh from behind.
'Pooh?' He whispered.

'Yes, Piglet?'

'Nothing,' said Piglet, taking Pooh's hand.
'I just wanted to be sure of you.'

—A.A. Milne, *Winnie- the-Pooh*

The next big step and big expense was our home study. The State of Tennessee requires adoptive parents to complete an official home study. Conducted by Mark, our licensed social worker, our home study involved more paperwork, individual interviews with Jeff, Houston, and me, a simple home tour and inspection, and finalization of our fee agreement. Again, our marriage was tested. The home study cost $1,500. I had remarkably pinched away $1,800.

The same week we were ready to call Mark to schedule our first home study visit, a golf buddy called Jeff and invited him to play Bandon Dunes Golf Resort in Bandon, Oregon.

Jeff loves golf and this was a once-in-a-lifetime opportunity as Bandon Dunes is world-famous. Their website boasts the course "is true to the spirit of Scotland's ancient links" and "golf as it was meant to be." How could my plan for expense and interviews compete with that?

Our home study, like my master plan, was meant to be deferred. I was furious but cautious. I love Jeff, and he had done all those essays (Big Chicked or not), answered hundreds of questions, consoled me a million times, and was an attentive, affectionate father to Houston. I did not want Jeff to resent me. Mark told us of one couple who actually divorced while they were waiting for a baby. I did not want my ambition to obstruct a wonderful opportunity for Tall Child. Also, this was a stellar opportunity for me to garner marital equity, which could prove quite useful in the future!

The trip cost $1,800. It took every penny I had saved.

I remember whining to my mother about my misfortune and she counseled, "Jody, you have to take care of Jeff and Houston's happiness because you *do* have them and they love you." I tossed myself daily pity parties by indulging in Starbucks *every* afternoon that Jeff was in Oregon. I was happy for Jeff but sad that I could not hurriedly climb the next adoption step. Jeff had a blast and sent me pictures of the golf course and its ocean views.

A few months passed and one night, I prayed to God, "Please help me come up with that money again." The next morning, I woke up and this exact thought came into my head: *Borrow against the life insurance policy.*

I called New York Life, extracted funds from the cash value in my policy, and went to the mailbox four days later to pull out the check that would pay for our home study. February 4, 2009, Houston and I, again, traipsed down to the Bethany office with documents and a fat check in hand. Mark congratulated us on finally completing everything on the checklist.

I wrote in the baby's journal on February 5.

Dear Baby,

How I love you even now and don't even know you yet! I'm waiting for Daddy and Houston to get home from basketball practice and I just made a new chocolate dessert that Judy and Grandmama promise is "out of this world." I paid for our home study yesterday. Mark will finish everything and file us as "fit" parents in the State of Tennessee. After that, we can get you any day! Sometimes I lose faith. I worry and think I'll never get you. I want you so much. Our first interviews are next week. I can't wait to meet you!
Love,
Mama

On March 26, 2009, I wrote again.

Dear Baby,

We are getting close! Mark came to our house March 16 at 3:00 p.m., and he stayed two hours to do our final home visit interview. I was a nervous wreck. Our house will NEVER be this clean again. I only mop for in-laws and social workers! I held Buzz so he wouldn't bark. Mark checked to see if we had a fire extinguisher, first aid supplies, smoke detectors, etc. I had just changed the batteries and was so embarrassed when the smoke detector in the guest room didn't work! Our first aid "kit" is scattered around the house. You should have seen your daddy scrambling to find hydrogen peroxide and Band-aids. I think Mark was messing with him! Houston took Mark on a tour. He showed him his Alamo fort outside. They shot Nerf basketball in the basement. Houston took Mark to your room and said, "This will be our baby's room."

Mark complimented Houston's behavior. Whew! We passed inspection! Daddy and I went through forms and questions with Mark. We signed the fee and services agreement. We hope you'll come from Tennessee, but you could come from anywhere in the USA. Annie is saving us her Sky Miles. That will be a huge financial help if we need to travel.

We are one step closer to finding you! Mark said he should finish our home study and be able to start showing our profile to birthparents in MAY!
Love,
Mama

For Mother's Day, Houston made me a card. Without having been prompted by his teacher, he drew and colored three stick figures in descending height: blue for Jeff, pink for me, and gray for Houston. He added a little round face with yellow hair floating above the three of us.

Even Houston sensed the ethereal nature of the wait for our baby.

On May 13 we celebrated Jeff's 46th birthday. Later that month, we had even more to celebrate when we opened a letter from Mark.

Dear Mr. and Mrs. Dyer,

I am pleased to inform you that your domestic adoption Home Study has been completed and it has been determined that your family meets the State of Tennessee requirements to be approved as an adoptive home. You are officially an "approved and waiting" domestic adoptive family. Welcome aboard!
Blessings,
Mark Akers, M.S.

Two Days, Two years, Two Never?

Now faith is the assurance of things hoped for,
the conviction of things not seen.

—Hebrews 11:1

Of course, I blasted an email to all.

Jeff and I are officially approved for adoption! We were approved exactly one year to the date of our formal application submission (May 21). I'm sure many of you are weary of my tale since I've been "trying" now for 7 years. I appreciate how you've listened to me, encouraged me, and most of all, prayed for me. Technically, we could get a baby any day now! During Houston's infant dedication our pastor said that children are not the possessions of their parents but belong to God. If we do someday have another child, she will belong to God and all of us because it will have taken God and all of us to get her here! Won't that be a wonderful day? I love you all.
Now, we simply wait...

I told the devoted prayer committee at Sequoyah Presbyterian Church the encouraging news. They celebrated our progress and promised to keep praying for us each week.

When my Uncle Dan heard the news, he called my mother so he could begin worrying in detail—this is a family flaw.

My mother asked him, "Dan, do you think we will love this baby immediately?"

He replied, "Donna! How much do you love a newborn beagle puppy? Of course we will! I met Jeff when he was thirty-five years old and I love that nut! How do you think we'll feel about a *baby*?"

Now What Do We Do?

I've learned that waiting is the most difficult bit,
and I want to get used to the feeling,
knowing that you're with me,
even when you're not by my side.

—Paolo Coehlo

In one of the Waiting Families group meetings, a waiting mother asked if it is okay to create and decorate a baby nursery. Terri, the agency director, said, "Do what your heart allows you to do regarding preparation for the baby's arrival."

Recall that I began trying to get pregnant when Houston was only nine months old. Each month after that was a conception guessing game, so I kept most of Houston's baby gear.

One weekend afternoon, three-year old Houston was napping away in his crib, or so I thought. I was washing dishes and talking on the phone when I looked out the kitchen sink window to see Houston dragging a baseball bat up the hill in the backyard. He had sneaked out of the house while I thought he was asleep. I did not even know he could get out of the baby bed. I installed a deadbolt that required a key to open it on the backdoor and rolled his crib into his closet.

Years later, around pregnancy test number forty, I became distraught. I had what Jeff calls a " major meltdown," over yet another negative result. In the "depths of despair" (as Pippi Longstocking might say) and a hormonal rage, I wheeled the baby bed out of Houston's closet, broke it apart, and angrily threw rails, slats, and wheels down the basement steps. When he got home, Jeff surveyed the damage and gently teased me about my meltdown. He hugged me and consoled me and picked up the pieces, storing them safely in the basement laundry room.

When I opened Mark's approval letter, I regained hope and confidence. I also felt more like the adoption would actually happen and I would need the crib, so I calmly reassembled the bed, and placed it in the hall bedroom, right beside Houston's, against a wall facing a large window that overlooks the backyard. Some waiting mothers have a tough time walking by an empty baby bed but little by little, sometimes hesitantly and feeling a little foolishly, I created the baby's nursery. Friends who saw the uninhabited room hosting a white wooden baby crib probably thought I was nuts, but were kind enough to ignore or complement the expanding infant-centered décor. I usually asked visitors, "Would you like to see the museum to my unknown child?"

The nursery served as a comfort to me and a tangible testimony of my faith to others. It served as proof that I anticipated my adopted child with confidence and joy. Mark calls adoption the "Ultimate Faith Journey." He is right. Doubt and fear are part of the process, but faith in thought *and* action are essential for survival.

THE QUESTION

If you are in the adoption process already, you know *The Question*: "Have you heard anything?"

After asking so many people to help you and pray for you, it is awful not to be able to give them hope, with some answer to *The Question*.

My buddy Stevens called and asked me *The Question* and I said, "No news, sorry."

She said, "Well, when you get your baby, I'm going to make you a ground beef casserole, but I don't want to buy the meat too early. Should I just buy some and freeze it?"

I answered, "You'd better hold off."

Months into our wait, she called again and asked, "Hey, have you heard anything?" I apologetically told her I had no news. She sighed, "Well, ground beef is on sale at Kroger, and I was going to buy some, but I guess I'll wait." This became a running, but comforting, joke.

Jeff and I had the privilege of education through Bethany, and I studied domestic adoption and legal risk placement. Friends and relatives only knew what we shared with them. You may tell everyone everything as you wait, or you may keep it all secret. It is up to you. Reasonable people will understand. But you had better figure out some response to *The Question* because you will hear it over and over again!

THE WAIT

I know an adoptive mother who got a baby boy through Bethany two days after her home study was approved. I am a typical overachiever and I really wanted (truthfully, I kind of expected) to be one of those lucky "drop from the sky baby" mothers who submits paperwork and within days or weeks gets a phone call from the social worker and has to make a fantastic and frantic run to Wal-Mart for all things baby. Two months dragged by. I wrote to the baby in July 2009.

Dear Baby,

You could come from anywhere in America, but I think you are coming straight from Heaven! Sometimes this wait feels impossible to endure. Yesterday Houston and I we went to a children's clothing store. He got mad when I wouldn't buy you an outfit. I don't know how big or how old you will be. He's only 7 ½ so he doesn't understand. He reminded me he was picking out the bathtub. We drove to Target, parked in the sacred spot (ha! ha!), and Houston bought you a big blue tub shaped like a whale with black eyes and a tail. It's called "Whale of a Tub."

You will have so much fun with Houston and your cousins Dan, Grady, Rosalind, Lawson, and Oliver. Casey, Ashley, and Betsy (thank goodness, I was

terrified she would not get pregnant and she has
wanted to be a mama her whole life), are pregnant! I
am the oldest cousin, and I am tired of them lapping me
in the baby race! You should have been the third baby
born in that crowd. I need to catch up! I have hope.
And, I have a little secret. I've prayed for you for years.
It's tough to filter my thoughts but sometimes I think I
hear that "still quiet voice" when I pray. On July 4th, I
was feeling sorry for myself, and I asked, "God, am I
EVER going to get this baby? I am so tired."
I heard, "She is on her way."
Love,
Mama

Team Adoption

For where two or three are gathered
together in my name,
there am I in the midst of them.

—Matthew 18:20

As days, weeks, and months passed, I kept busy with my teaching courses, Houston's schoolwork, and Houston's sports, including his fall flag football team. That was a really sweet time in our wait. I learned how to anticipate God's gifts and see how all of our lives intertwine.

Jeff coached Houston's flag football team. I call it Team Adoption because we mothers were our own sort of informal adoption squad. Talania has two sons through domestic adoption. Laura, the one with the "paper cuts" t-shirt, has an adopted daughter from China and was waiting for her son Luke from Ethiopia. Amy was working toward internationally adopting two brothers, and player Ethan's aunt was working with a local birthmother to hopefully bring home a son at the end of football season. And, of course, Coach Dyer was adopted and waiting for a baby!

Ethan's aunt's story played out week by week as did our football game schedule. She lives in another part of Tennessee, but the baby's birthmother lived in a small town near Knoxville. Each week, she and her husband came to our game and the birthmother's OB/GYN appointment. I was a nervous wreck for her and knew my time on the block was coming, at least I hoped so. By the way, she got her baby.

Another Bite

September 17, 2009, I wrote in the baby's journal.

Dear Baby,

I am not sure what to think. Yesterday would have been Grandmama and Granddaddy Scott's wedding anniversary. I was getting Houston dressed for baseball practice and reading Janeen's twins' baby shower invitation when the phone rang. It was Mark! He told me about a birthmother in the Tri-Cities area who wanted to see profiles. Both birthparents are college students (just like Daddy's were). They want adoptive parents who like UT football, have only one or no children, appreciate rural living, and they want a stay-at-home mother. Usually, Mark doesn't call waiting families until a birthmother actually chooses them and asks to meet them. Mark called me because he thinks we'd be a great match, but the birthmother is pregnant with twins—one girl and one boy! So, he had to get our permission to show her our profile.

I called your daddy and asked, with my fingers-crossed, "How much do you love me?" He said, "More than anything in the world."

I told him about the situation, and to my surprise and elation, he said, "Go ahead!" I think when he heard "little baby boy" he couldn't resist. I called Mark right back.

I am excited! You may have to share your room. The birthmother is due in December. She may decide to parent (keep the babies), the extended family may blow the deal, all the usual risks are there; plus, with twins, placement is less likely, statistically. The important thing is we are in the running! This is the second time we've had a chance for twins. Could there be two of you? We'll see!
Love,
Mama

Doubling Down

If we brought home these twins, I would have my daughter *and* another son. These twins presented a crucial opportunity. I knew deep down that Jeff and I would not have the money, strength, or youth to endure the adoption process twice. I kept thinking about how this incredible chance would complete my plan for three children. Jeff, Houston, and I were scheduled to meet the birthparents the following week.

Here came fierce winds of worry. All along, in any given situation, we intended to spare Houston any stress until the last reasonable moment. But, because these birthparents wanted to meet Houston, we had to tell him about the opportunity. I thought he would have a million questions but he did not. He took the news and stress in stride.

I fretted over what to wear to meet my twins' birthmother. I wanted to look cheerful but not dorky, competent but not dull, motherly but not matronly. She liked rural living, so I could not look too citified. No problem—I am "country," remember. I chose brown slacks, a modest plaid camisole and a turquoise cardigan. I splurged on a manicure and pedicure, and I bought the birthmother a gift box from Bath & Body Works. For an hour, I wavered between lotions, soaps, and body wash. I eventually selected relaxing aromas and avoided anything alluding to sex or romance.

I informed the store clerks about my upcoming "interview," and they were fascinated. Had I stayed longer at West Town Mall in my weak state I might have allowed those kiosk people to curl my hair and whiten my teeth! I was going to be completely preoccupied until I met those birthparents. I pressed my new outfit, wrapped the gift in a colorful, not my usual Dollar Tree cheapo gift bag, crafted a note on a pretty card, and daydreamed.

Man to Mouse. Pink To Blue?

My motto was always to keep swinging.
Whether I was in a slump or feeling badly
or having trouble off the field,
the only thing to do was keep swinging.
                                        —Hank Aaron

The birthmother pregnant with twins did not choose us. We never even met her.

A few days before our scheduled meeting, she called her social worker and said she had found out through word-of-mouth that a friend was trying to adopt. The friend had just begun adoption paperwork. Understandably, the birthmother felt more comfortable placing her children with someone she knew. When Mark called and explained, I was sad. Jeff was disappointed, but admitted he was relieved because he was a little nervous about bringing home two babies. Houston was furious. I told him what had happened, and he said, "Those people haven't even finished their papers. We have. That's not fair."

I marveled at how I had won and lost two separate chances at twins. As Mark and Terri suggested, I turned my thoughts toward the twins' birthparents and the chosen adoptive parents. I took the bag of gifts to the Bethany office and asked Bunny, the office coordinator, to give them to the twins' birthmother. Bunny said, "How sweet of you, Jody. That's just bread on the water, honey." Did she mean like fishing bait or is that a Biblical reference? Either way, it was funny and comforting. This was all in September 2009.

Interestingly, as I daydreamed about those twins, I mostly thought about the little boy. In October, Houston and I spent the night with Cousins Leah and Oliver. Oliver was nine months old at the time. We were relaxing and drinking red wine on Leah's patio in Gatlinburg, and Oliver was swaying in his red and blue Little Tikes swing. At the summit of each forward swing, Houston clumsily spooned a dollop of applesauce into Oliver's open mouth. I watched in amusement their awkward efforts, and thought, *Would I say no to this little boy combo? No.* Two weeks later, for a school project, Houston's buddy Baker wrote about his friend Houston and their plan to become professional football players together. The following Wednesday night, fellow church member and Bethany mom Bonnie asked me *The Question.* I filled her in on the latest let down, and she told me "You will get exactly who you are supposed to have."

I reflected on these events and words for days and kept thinking to myself, *I am a good "boy mama." I love little boys. We have so much fun with Houston's friends and teammates. I would love to have a daughter, but God knows the right soul for our family.*

I asked Jeff how he felt about us changing our Bethany paperwork to say we had no preference between a boy or girl. Jeff is a natural athlete who coaches youth sports. Houston is all boy, in constant motion, and was already playing three sports at seven years old.

I joked to Jeff, "You know that if we change this paperwork we're going to get a short little boy who doesn't like sports. Will you be a good band parent?"

The conversation reminded me of one Jeff's parents had with their social worker in 1963. The social worker explained that Jeff may excel in sports and asked if they (neither one is an athlete) would support his "natural" inclination to play basketball or baseball. Ironic. The Dyers' caseworker said, "We are looking for a home for the baby, not a baby for the home." Jeff played high school and junior college basketball and his parents never missed a game.

Anyway, after my usual fretting fistful of questions, a frustrated Jeff said, "You are getting on my nerves. Call Mark." So, I stepped out of my own way and changed our paperwork and profile to say girl *or* boy. That evening, I wrote.

> *Dear Baby,*
> *Baby, if you are a boy, I don't ever want you to feel you were a second choice. Maybe my timing and bullheadedness about wanting a girl is just another deferment. I want you to understand that you are being chosen, fought for, and cried over. I have put my body, marriage, finances, and friends through you-know-what. You are special. I am going to buy something blue.*
> *Love,*
> *Mama*

I had already decorated the nursery, a little bit, in feminine décor. A huge tobacco basket hung over the full-sized bed next to the baby crib. Weeks before I had fastened an eighteen-inch-wide vivid pink paper zinnia in the center of the time-hewn, grayish brown, barnwood basket. Two significant dolls from my childhood rested in the white wood railed baby crib. My maternal grandmother, Freddy, hand-made each of her seven granddaughters a doll. My doll, Penny, perched in the white crib alongside the Little Red Riding Hood Topsy Turvy doll my paternal grandmother, Wimmie, had given me. As promised in the journal entry, I purchased something blue. I found a dark green gingham pillow. A quilted navy blue rectangle sewn across the front framed a cream corduroy elephant. I brought the pillow home and set it on the full sized bed, underneath the tobacco basket and its pink blossom.

I told Houston about our decision to welcome a boy baby into our family, and we talked about names again. Houston said that if we got a girl, Hattie was not a good name. Instead, we should call her Petunia because I like flowers. I told him we would name a boy after my daddy, Scott. He insisted we call the boy Scotty because that sounded more like a baby. After we made the change to pink *or* blue, I felt a small sense of loss, thinking I decreased my chances at a daughter. But, more strongly, I felt a boost, like we had taken positive action toward actually bringing home a child.

What saves a man is to take a step.
Then another step.

—C.S. Lewis, *A Grief Observed*

"Pregnant Women Are Smug"

*Everyone knows it, nobody says it
because they're pregnant.*

—Garfunkel and Oates

At that time, in addition to the post-graduate work at Lincoln Memorial University, I took three courses at Pellissippi State Technical Community College (PSTCC) to secure my teaching certificate. One class, Web Design, was an internet-based course where I learned to write hypertext markup language code and design web pages. When I registered for classes at UT my freshman year back in 1992, I did so in person in Thompson Boling Arena. Here I was twenty years later learning to write code. Fortunately, my Uncle Toby gave me an old computer he had stored in his work shed. Neighbor Allyn gave me a monitor. I later secured a printer from Jeff's work friend. My assortment of computer components (printer, screen, keyboard, and tower) was fifty shades of technology gray.

The web course was challenging for this middle-aged wife, mother to Houston, substitute teacher, and frantic hopeful adoptive parent. The detailed assignments required focus and concentration and my mind was everywhere. Sometimes I was not sure if I was doing homework or emailing the teacher. One day, almost in tears because my photo only showed on my website as a little red box in big white square, I called the web teacher on the phone. To my astonishment and embarrassment, her voice undulated like that of a seventy-year-old woman. She calmed me down granny-style and I thought, *Someone older than my mother just explained HTML code to me. I need to catch up to the rest of the world.*

Luckily, the other two Pellissippi classes were held in traditional classrooms. The small open-enrollment school's student body consists mostly of eighteen to twenty-two year olds. I was the oldest student in both of those classes. When I walked through the parking lots and campus, I habitually inspected the young crowd for pregnant girls without wedding bands, just as I did in my gynecologist's waiting room. I would have been bold enough to strike up a conversation with a pregnant student or patient, but I never got the opportunity.

I saw no pregnancy at Pellissippi, and the girls at the gynecologist's office always had mothers or boyfriends with them.

When I was not baby-hunting, I focused on my coursework. In one class, *Communications in an Information Age,* I learned the history of recorded information and communication, from Sequoyah's Cherokee alphabet to Zuckerberg's Facebook. Our news writer-turned-professor led class discussions on technology's impact on law, industry, culture, and ethics.

I had a Facebook account, but I did not use it much. Most of the posts I saw from others were boastful and self-aggrandizing and grossed me out, like an Internet version of "My kid made the honor roll" bumper stickers.

My favorites were (are) what I call "declarations of love" ('# years ago today, I married the greatest person in the whole wide world'), "Betty Crocks" (photos of home cooked meals), and "brag books" (pink pedicures in white sand before blue waves). I think I will have a photographer take my picture as I cook one of those beef dishes where the critter's bones are upright and wrapped in foil party hats and the dessert requires a small propane torch, *on* the beach, *with* a pedicure, next to my version of the greatest husband in the world.

When I waited tables at IHOP the summer of my father's death, I had what *7 Habits* author Stephen Covey calls a paradigm shift. I would watch customers happily banter and pass the syrup while I wrapped spoons, forks, and knives in paper napkins the IHOP way, thinking all the time *I can't believe my daddy is gone. My life really sucks. I am miserable. How are my mama and I ever going to feel normal or happy again?* I realized that, regardless of their outward show, many people are in overwhelming, debilitating personal pain. The shift stuck permanently. I always tip twenty percent, no matter what the service is like, and I can even cut my friends a lot of slack when they claim contentment on Facebook.

My next comment may infuriate some folks, but this book is written for those who have suffered or are suffering through the rigors of infertility and/or adoption. I adore my friends' children, and I love my cousins' children like my own, but "belly pics" are painful images that are often forced on infertile, childless, sometimes grieving couples.

Anyone who has dealt with infertility intimately understands the magical common miracle of pregnancy. An infertile person is likely thrilled for expecting families, but when she logs into Facebook and up pops a fat happy belly, or worse, an ultrasound picture, she feels a virtual slap in the face. To protect my mental state through the adoption process, I simply "hid" pregnant friends from my timeline page.

Adoption in the Age of Mass Media

The Internet has always been,
and always will be,
a magic box.

—Marc Andreessen

Thanks to my Pellissippi classes, I gained a greater grasp of what social media could do to *help* me and took a positive second look at Facebook. I logged in with new vigor, realizing two things: One, I could respectfully track and learn from successful adoptive couples. Two: I could use social media to promote my cause.

I reached out to Bethany mom Valerie, whom I stalked via Facebook. She had recently brought home an infant son, and I loved to look at their happy photos. I emailed her for advice. She responded.

Jody,
Thank you for the congrats, and I am glad that [our story] gives you hope. Waiting is not easy at all. We waited 18 months and had a few bumps and one failed

placement, so I know what you mean with all the emotions. Adoption is not for the weak and is definitely not the "easy way." I will tell you what I wish someone had told me. Don't worry – you are not going insane. *I think a couple of times my husband thought that I was losing it. Once, on the way home from church, I just bawled because one of the girls in the class told us she was pregnant. I was happy for her but it felt as if someone had pulled my heart out, twisted and stomped on it, then put it back in. I don't know exactly how you have been feeling, but if you do ever start feeling that way (or any other way) don't worry. It's normal. On a positive note though, you will eventually have a new baby. You just have to hang in there. Don't give up. Once we got [our child] it felt as if the wait really had not been that long, and he was totally worth it.*

On my profile page, I posted a "promotional" message that Jeff and I were approved and waiting for a baby. I also attached a link from both our Facebook accounts to our Bethany webpage, hoping to exponentially increase our odds of finding a baby. What I did find out was that adoption stories were all around me and I never knew.

I reconnected with two of my best childhood buddies. The three of us went to Pigeon Forge Elementary School from kindergarten through eighth grade together, but I had lost touch with them since high school. Michelle saw my post and explained to me how she found her son through adoption at none other than Bethany Christian Services five years earlier. Tobi is an artist who also custom creates baby gifts, clothing, and accessories. Sometime in December, I saw her work on Facebook through a mutual friend's page. I "friended" her and messaged her saying that I was waiting for a baby through adoption and wanted to order something special from her.

Tobi messaged back that she, too, was trying to adopt, and had suffered several failed efforts. I could not believe we were both in the same rocky adoption boat!

In addition to Facebook, I kept tabs on Bethany's waiting families. I developed a method. Every day, I checked the Bethany website, where our profile, along with hundreds of others, was cataloged.

I clicked the *"Adoption, discover more"* link, then the *"Meet families waiting to adopt"* link to see a vertical inventory of hundreds of thumbnail family photos. Adjacent to each photo was the beginning of that family's "Dear Birthparent" letter. (Today, October 4, 2012, as I type this, there are seven hundred eighty two families on that list.) I then used the drop down box under *"Select a State"* to narrow my field of study to Tennessee families.

Bethany uses the term "Placement Pending" when a baby has been born and placed with an adoptive family, but the birthparents' rights are not yet legally terminated. When an adoptive family has a placement pending, Bethany's webmaster fogs their photo and enters in italics *Placement Pending* to the right of their names. I scrolled through Tennessee families, eagerly searching for foggy photos. When I found one, if I knew the family through the Suffer Club, I Facebook "friended" the mother.

I do not know why I waited to befriend folks until after a placement. I wish I had reached out more in the group meetings and formed bonds early on with the other mothers. I think I kept my distance because I really never knew what that parent was going through and the adoption process is innately surrounded with secrecy and mystery. Regardless, I now had a bird's eye view to an array of possible adoption stories that mine could mimic. I lived and learned vicariously through other adoptive mothers.

Christmas came and I continued to answer *The Question* with "No, no news."

I was feeling pretty somber when I performed my daily check on the Bethany Waiting Families website and saw a message from Mark. He wrote a Christmas greeting for all waiting families. In summary, it read as follows:

Since I've been at Bethany, I've learned more than ever that our very lives are a "faith journey" and the adoption journey is... often very uncertain and unpredictable.... My prayer is that God will fulfill the desires of your heart in 2010...time and time again I have seen God bring 'the right children to the right families in the right time in the right way.' We are blessed to have you as part of our family at Bethany. Keep praying for our birthmothers, birthfathers, and Bethany staff as they minister daily to those whom God has entrusted to us.
Blessings and Peace to You,
Mark

Mark posted the message just weeks after two of my cousins delivered their babies. Two more were getting close to their due dates. Mark came through again with the much-needed reassurance that we waiting mothers needed to hear.

I gleefully observed the mothers from Houston's flag football team post beautiful pictures of their sons from Tennessee and Ethiopia. I kept a vigilant eye on the Bethany website but could not deduce a mathematical formula for *Placement Pending* notifications. Even so, each time I saw one, I celebrated and grew in confidence that I, too, would see that prized label next to Jeff and Jody Dyer.

Food City Baby

Christmas passed. A week or so later, I was grocery shopping at Food City when my buddy Renee, a front-end manager there, said, "Hey! I need to ask you something. One of our cashiers is pregnant and wants to give the baby up for adoption. Would you like to talk to her?"

I thought to myself, *Stay calm. Where is she? Where is she?* The Food City birthmother was not at work, so I got as much information as I could from Renee, which was not much. The birthmother was due in July. She was seventeen, a high school senior, and already enrolled to attend college in the fall. Her sister had placed a baby two years before.

I left Food City with Houston's snacks and my strategy: I would do lots of grocery shopping until I "just happened to land" in the pregnant cashier's lane. A few trips into the plan, it happened!

Waiting parents, if you have never talked to a real live birthmother, let me prepare you. You may be a wreck; you may be in awe; you may feel that every single word rolling off your tongue sinks like a cast iron anchor (that was me). Above all, be yourself. You are fragile and real. Birthmothers are also fragile and real.

I broke into a cold sweat when I pushed my cart into her lane. I awkwardly introduced myself to the young, beautiful, imperceptibly pregnant cashier, saying, "I am friends with Renee. I am trying to adopt a baby so she told me about your pregnancy."

Luckily, no one got behind me in line, so we had time to talk. To my surprise, the cashier completely opened up to me. She explained the birthfather situation, which, from an adoption standpoint, presented a significant challenge and would require DNA testing *after* the child's birth. This seventeen-year-old girl's mother kicked her out of their home, so she moved in with her elderly grandfather. She went to high school during the day and worked at Food City nights and weekends to help her grandfather pay rent and utilities. She also told me her sister's baby's adoptive parents had been a huge disappointment. They were not keeping their original promise to allow contact between her sister and her child. She explained she wanted to do a private placement and not use an adoption agency.

Jeff and I wanted to use Bethany, not only for many positive reasons, but also because of our tight financial situation. Bethany's Knoxville office has a structured fee agreement that is based on income level. Plus, once we finalized our fee agreement with Bethany, any additional costs accrued during the adoption process would be absorbed by Bethany. As I understand it, Bethany offices decide such procedures on the local office level. Adoptive parents should make sure to research the precise pricing and payment structures for different agencies and offices within those agencies.

Through generous benefactors and successful fundraising, the *Knoxville* Bethany office is able to subsidize adoption costs, while many agencies and attorneys require adoptive parents to pay the additional expenses, often called "pass-through costs."

There are no refunds of pass-through costs, so if we, say, helped this young girl with her rent, car payment, medical bills, and counseling, and she changed her mind and did not give us the baby, we were through, financially speaking. We could not afford a second attempt at adoption if this placement failed. There were other issues in this situation that I must keep private out of respect for the birthmother and her child. Because of those confidential details, the unpredictability of pass-through costs, and the discouraging birthfather scenario, I sorrowfully knew this was not my baby.

When I left the store, I plopped into the safety and privacy of my car, and, for a long time, ruminated over each thing she told me. I questioned my gut reaction, but when I talked with Jeff, his response matched mine.

Some might ask, "Why did you pass on such an opportunity when you were so desperate all those years?" It is hard to explain reasoning in adoption. The gut-wrenching, almost mystical process can be confusing. Though painful, it is completely normal for an adoptive family to pass on an opportunity. Spiritual things, ideas, and attitudes are intangible but crucial when making such life-altering decisions. Adoption situations are like mirages, except, now and then, the water *is* there. But the first opportunity you find may belong to someone else.

I thought about the kind cashier, the details of her situation, and called my friend Tobi.

I relayed to Tobi every single detail of the cashier's story. Tobi and her husband, like the cashier's sister, had endured a bad experience with an agency and had since contracted an adoption attorney to help them. Tobi's resources and approach were a beautiful fit for the situation. To my delight, after hearing everything, Tobi was interested.

As former UT football coach Phil Fulmer would say, I was "fired up and focused" on my friend's behalf. A few days later, I visited Food City to talk to the cashier. Once we were customer free, I gently explained to the understanding cashier how I was not a match for her baby, but that my friend was looking to adopt.

I asked if Tobi could contact her. The cashier agreed and wrote her email address and phone number on a piece of register tape. I passed the contact information along to Tobi, and that story was set to motion.

As Tobi's relationship with the cashier began, I waited. I had been on the baby quest since 2002 and the adoption journey since 2008. Just two years before Houston had told his principal, "I'm getting a baby when I'm eight years old." I sure hoped he was right. He turned eight on January 8, 2010.

Phone Call

January 20, 2010, I wrote to the baby.

Dear Baby,
We've been officially approved and waiting eight months tomorrow. That's awfully close to nine months. Anyway, I was at the grocery store this morning and my cell phone rang. I looked at the caller I.D. and saw "Mark Akers!" I said "Hello."

He asked how Houston and Jeff were, etc. and then added, "Well, I need to see you guys again. I have another situation to talk to you about. I have a birthmother who liked your profile and wants to meet you."

I was standing right by the bananas and I almost went bananas!

I asked, "What can you tell me?"

He said, "We'll talk about everything tomorrow."

"Can you tell me if it's a boy or girl?"

He said, "I don't think we know... let me look at the paperwork...yes, we do know... I'll tell you tomorrow."

I suppose social workers need to have some fun.

I am nervous *and excited. I hope this is the real deal. I called Grandmama, and she started her Aunt Pitty-Pat routine, and I told her to keep her big mouth under control. Houston is sick and staying home from school tomorrow so Grandmama is coming tomorrow to watch him while Daddy and I meet with Mark. I am skipping class. We'll take no chances missing that meeting!*

We have new babies in the family; just before Christmas, Beau and Little Toby were born. Betsy's and Jill's babies will be here in March, and Kellie Ann is pregnant. It is tough to hear all that good news and have to rely strictly on faith to anticipate my child. I feel sorry for myself sometimes, but I would not trade this experience for any of theirs. This journey has grown my faith, given my marriage greater depth, and taught me invaluable lessons that are bound to make me a better mama to Houston and *you. You are worth every sad /happy/anxious/strange moment.*
I love you.
Mama

East Tennessee *Juno*

We met with Mark on January 21. He prayed with us and then explained all he knew of the birthparents' backgrounds and medical history. The baby was due May 21, 2010. We learned the birthmother's name was Kerri, and the birthfather's name was Bryant. Mark told us Kerri was twenty-one years old, five feet one inch tall, from Knoxville, and outgoing. Bryant was twenty years old, five feet seven inches tall, from Pennsylvania, smart, and funny. I tuned in carefully when Mark teasingly asked us to guess the child's sex.

"A boy?"

Mark confirmed my guess.

I smiled at Jeff, "There's your short little boy!"

From Mark's description the birthparents' intentions sounded solid, but there were some risks. First, Kerri and Bryant were still a couple. What if he asked her to marry him? Second, Bryant lived in Pennsylvania and Kerri lived in Tennessee. Was there a chance she would move to be with Bryant? Third, several of Kerri and Bryant's family members either did not know about the adoption plan or were against it. Could they convince Kerri and Bryant to parent?

Mark advised us to prayerfully consider the situation and meet the birthmother. I was not sure I had the strength to meet with such a special person and then possibly say "no" to her if we felt the placement risks were too great.

I had a surprising and overwhelming fear, now that a serious opportunity existed, that I would make the wrong decision. Jeff and I leaned on Mark, who counseled, "Always meet a birthmother."

We arranged to meet Kerri on Friday, January 29.

Along with nervous tension, January 29 brought a big snow. I panicked that Kerri would not be able to get to the meeting and we would have another few days or another week of anticipation. I called Mark who assured Kerri was excited about meeting us and would be there. Houston's school was closed for snow so neighbor Allyn graciously entertained Houston so we could go to the Bethany office.

ACT 1: They meet

We sat in Mark's office as Mark explained what we should expect. I had a list of questions— nerdy, but helpful at such an anxious time. Mark cheerfully said, "Well, let's go to the little living room and wait for Kerri and her mom." When I walked out of Mark's office, I looked down a long gray hallway and saw a petite young girl wearing skinny jeans, a black zip-up hoodie, and Merrells carrying a Tinker Bell tote bag. She looked pregnant, but not far along.

There she is.

I met her uniquely light, wide eyes. Not knowing what else to do, I smiled at her. I felt tall, old, awkward, and ready as I followed Mark to the small living room at the front of the Bethany office building.

Kerri's social worker, Lauren, brought Kerri and Kerri's mother, Lynn, into the room through a different doorway, just after Jeff and I sat down. Mark led us in prayer in the small parlor. Jeff and I gave Kerri a vase full of bright yellow daises and a journal and colorful pens wrapped in a polka-dot gift bag. I had printed and pasted II Corinthians, Chapter 1, Verses 2-7 to the inside cover of the journal.

May God our Father and the Lord Jesus Christ give you grace and peace. All praise to God, the Father of our Lord Jesus Christ. God is our merciful Father and the source of all comfort. He comforts us in all our troubles so that we can comfort others. When they are troubled, we will be able to give them the same comfort God has given us. For the more we suffer for Christ, the more God will shower us with his comfort through Christ. Even when we are weighed down with troubles, it is for your comfort and salvation! For when we ourselves are comforted, we will certainly comfort you. Then you can patiently endure the same things we suffer. We are confident that as you share in our sufferings, you will share in the comfort God gives us.

Earlier that week, Mark had also described Kerri as "not easily offended." He encouraged me to ask questions, so I used my list. I asked Kerri about her childhood, school, and personal goals. Kerri was articulate, bright, and engaging. I love stories and interesting people. I respond to such characters, and I recognized immediately that this raven-haired wisp of a pregnant twenty-one year old with tilted gray eyes and enormous personality was most certainly a "character."

Who is this Girl?

After that, things moved
with swiftness and awkwardness both,
like something simultaneously strong and broken.

—Lorrie Moore, *A Gate at the Stairs, A Novel*

Kerri entertained us with stories of her eventful middle and high school years, fiery romances, and elaborate plans for her future. Lynn told us about Tanner, her pet West African Grey Parrot and Tizzie, Kerri's pet rat. Kerri revealed with great passion her interests in professional wrestling, major league baseball, everything *Twilight*, and British literature.

She called the baby London, explaining that she felt weird calling him "the baby" since he was in her body and she cared about him, so, as a devoted Anglophile, she named him after her favorite city. When I told her that Jeff's brother lives in London, England, she was moved.

When I boldly asked, "Why did you want to meet *us*?" Kerri painted with colorful words the connections and similarities she saw between us.

Growing up, Kerri had a Yorkshire terrier just like our Buzz. Like me, Kerri and Lynn are only children and wanted

London to have a sibling. She adored what Houston wrote in the "Dear Birthparent" letter, saying it was sweet and very touching. Kerri and Lynn expressed respect and intrigue toward Jeff's adoption. Kerri commented, "He will understand the baby better and can help him with any adoption issues."

She also liked how cheerful our house was in the profile pictures. She said it looked "comfortable and not uptight." The farm was "awesome" as were all the little boy cousins ready and willing to take on another playmate.

We learned as much as we could about each other in that two hour meeting. Kerri appeared intelligent, vibrant, personable, and tolerant. She seemed tough, with a strong sense of self, yet tenderhearted toward others. I liked her confidence and sense of humor.

She had soul.

I also liked her mother, Lynn, who was a bit younger than Jeff. Kerri and Lynn both told us that they knew we were special after looking at our book. They had time to digest all things Dyer because they had looked through our profile book, read our "Dear Birthparent" letters, and listened to Mark and Lauren describe our history, life, family, and future. In contrast, Jeff and I knew only what Mark had told us of Kerri and Bryant's backgrounds.

As Lynn continuously complimented us, it dawned on me that she and Kerri were concerned about *us* liking *them*. But birthmothers are the Holy Grail of promise. Waiting adoptive parents, at least the ones I know, reverently hold birthmothers in sky-high esteem. I felt sorry for Kerri and Lynn at that point and did everything I could to express my respect and admiration and put them at ease. Kerri and Lynn said they felt an instant connection to us. Mark was right; *always meet a birthmother*.

When Jeff and I got in the car after the meeting, we were reeling with thought and emotion. I asked him how he felt.

Jeff's left hand rested on the steering wheel and his right hand turned the key in the ignition. He looked contemplatively in the rear-view mirror as he backed out of our parking spot and declared, "That was one of the greatest experiences of my life."

When Houston is really happy or excited about something, he loses control of his smile. He can not close his mouth. He becomes self-conscious, with an unrelenting grin. My mother termed it "perking." Houston "perks" when he shoots a three-pointer, presents me with an "A" on his schoolwork, or his favorite TV show is about to come on. Jeff and I were smiling that same way. We felt something special and desperately tried to comprehend what had just occurred. When I got home, I wrote in the journal.

> *Dear Baby,*
> *We met a potential birthmother today, maybe yours. Her name is Kerri. She will meet with another couple this Friday. I promise you right now they are praying this is their baby. This is hard. Kerri showed me an ultrasound picture with a sweet little profile. This is VERY hard. To be completely honest, I would take this child in a heartbeat. I just don't know if I'm supposed to. As we wait for Kerri to meet with the other family, we will pray for her, the precious baby in that black and white sonogram, the other couple, and our peace of mind. If this is you, I love you! If not, I love you!*
> *Mama*

Purgatory

Late that afternoon Lauren (Kerri's counselor) called to tell us that Kerri was "madly in love" with us and refused to meet with the other couple.

I was terrified. We had to make a decision of incalculable importance and I did not know what to do. Though we really liked Kerri, we were still apprehensive about the situation and its likelihood of placement. If we said yes to Kerri's baby, we would be off "the list" of waiting families until Kerri's due date four months later. That is a long wait at that stage of the game; most birthparents choose an adoptive family in the last month of pregnancy. Plus, if we said "Yes," and Kerri kept the baby, we would have to come up with more money and renew our paperwork. Mark said that there were several birthmothers at Bethany at the time and that we were a "hot couple!" If we said "yes" to Kerri, we had a fifty percent chance of placement, no matter the situation. I think that all along I naively expected to meet a birthmother and feel one hundred percent certain of my decision.

I gave my mother all of the details and we took full advantage of the Verizon Wireless "Friends and Family Plan." Jeff the procrastinator said he had to think for a few days. Jeff's vulnerabilities, strengths, and temperament fully presented themselves in this interesting state of affairs.

I used to tease Jeff by telling everyone he was a cosmopolitan redneck. On Saturdays, he mowed the grass wearing a sweater vest. Once, only once, he wore a turtleneck to Thanksgiving with my family on our farm. We called him Sven for about a year.

Jeff is one of those guys who can get along with anyone. Like me, he is genuinely enamored by people who are unique. Instead of being annoyed or offended by differences, he is intrigued or, at the least, amused. He is sensitive toward others, except on the basketball court, and takes great pains to try to politely assimilate into any crowd. I often go to him for social advice.

When we met, he played softball with a crowd of blue-collar workers. He competed in a fantasy football league against all his teammates. Jeff and his softball friends often met on Saturday nights at a smoke-filled beer dive called Sonny's to trade players and talk trash.

Jeff would play golf all day at a country club with the fraternity boy businessmen crowd then go directly to Sonny's. If Jeff had on a sweater vest when he got to the bar, he would take it off and leave it in the car. He claimed he did not want to look snobby. I also think he was sparing himself a merciless round of harassment. Most of those guys wore uniforms to work and would have wet their pants laughing if he strolled in wearing one of his pro-shop purchased Ashworth V-neck sweaters.

Jeff, for the most part, has always seemed secure with being adopted.

His mother began telling him at a very young age about how he came into their family. When Jeff was five years old, he was riding in the backseat of his mother's station wagon. A little friend accompanied him. As Jeff's mother drove, she overheard the little boys' discussion.

Jeff said to his friend, "You know, I am adopted."

The friend asked, "What does that mean?"

Jeff explained, "It means I grew in my daddy's tummy instead of my mommy's."

Other than that funny instance, Jeff has always seemed to have a clear understanding and acceptance of his origin. But with adoption, insecurities are innate. Jeff, though very close to his parents, was not immune. After they adopted Jeff, Jeff's parents had biological children, Jenny and Jay. Jeff has told me that the one thing that drove him crazy growing up was when people remarked about how he did not look like any of his family members. Jeff's now graying hair was blonde his whole life. He is tall and lanky with a fair, ruddy complexion. The Dyers are average in height, with dark hair and skin, and have rounded physiques. I once warned Jeff to be careful not to stand third from the left in a family photo, else it would look like the Dyers were "shooting the bird"! With a summer tan, Jenny almost looks Greek. The only thing Greek about Jeff is the hell-raising legacy he left at the Sigma Chi fraternity house at The University of Tennessee.

Jeff's difference in appearance actually spurred his nickname, which dozens of friends still call him today. He played basketball at Hiwassee College in Madisonville, Tennessee. Of course, Mr. and Mrs. Dyer attended his first game (all of his games, actually). Excited to see his son's debut game, Mr. Dyer, then a Knoxville area banker, left his office, picked up Jeff's mother, and rushed to Hiwassee College. When he rolled up in front of the gym, Jeff's teammates watched as a five-foot-something, round-bellied businessman in a suit and tie followed polished loafers out of a huge blue Oldsmobile '98. When he saw Mr. Dyer step out of the big fancy car, one of the players yelled, "Dang man, Boss Hog's done come to our ballgame."

Mr. Dyer looked like a ribbon-cutting philanthropist there to present a poster board check at half-time, not the typical father of a college basketball player. When Jeff pointed out that the stout, round man was indeed his daddy, the boys ragged him endlessly. They started calling Jeff "Hog" and, as any great nickname does, it stuck.

So, here "Hog" was: tall, quiet, and almost fifty. A little league coach and golfer, he was considering adopting the child of a tiny, lyrical, very *different from him* young woman. I think he expected someone more like us. Someone who looked like him?

Kerri was young enough to be Jeff's daughter. In our meeting, she showed us one of her tattoos. Jeff gawked at an ink on skin version of "Nature's first green is gold" from Robert Frost and politely squeezed out, "Yeah, that's nice." Jeff is not a fan of tattoos or poetry.

The feminine, soft-voiced Kerri imparted to Jeff all the attributes of her favorite alternative rock artists. She spoke with affection and detail about her pet rat. Jeff listened and absorbed and, though he was very sweet to Kerri, kept pretty quiet in our meeting. He was quiet at home that weekend, too.

The ever-patient Mark called Monday and asked, "So, have you made a decision? What are you guys thinking right now?"

I said, "You were absolutely right. We should have met her. That was an incredible experience. We are not sure we are ready to say 'yes' just yet. I am leaning toward 'yes,' but Jeff needs more time."

I listed all the sources of our apprehension and jokingly added, "I think Jeff is trying hard to make a decision, but he's distracted by the pet rat."

Mark chuckled and coached, "I understand your concerns. But, keep in mind two things. One, environment is everything. Tell Jeff that if you adopt this baby, he will be a Dyer, and he won't have a pet rat! Your child will inherit unique traits from his birth family, but he will also like baseball and basketball because Houston does. Two, placement is *always* fifty-fifty, but I think this is a good situation for you guys. There is no way to ever be sure. Saying "yes" to *any* opportunity requires a big leap of faith, and, sometimes, you just have to jump."

You just have to jump. That was all I needed to hear. I wanted to commit, Grandmama was already raring to go, but "Hog" had to think.

I believe now, looking back and remembering that pensive week, that Jeff's thoughts went beyond meeting Kerri on a Friday in January 2010. I think my tender-hearted husband was trying to reconcile something that happened in May 1963.

He was thinking about the birthmother who *did* look like him.

The Leap of Faith

For time is the longest distance between two places.

—Tennessee Williams, *The Glass Menagerie*

Mark and I waited for Jeff. I submitted to the will of my husband. Yep. I sure did. There is no "meeting in the middle" with adoption. Decisions *must* be unanimous.

Friday, February 4, Mark called for our answer.

We told him, "Yes."

I felt as though Jeff and I had, hand in hand, leapt off a cliff into deep, tumultuous, yet promising waters, and we would not see land for four months. We would tread water in a storm of emotions and decision-making. I hung up the phone and walked into the "museum to the unknown child." I leaned over the baby crib railing and laid my face, chest, and arms across the green and white polka dot sheeted mattress (raised to accommodate a newborn). I envisioned a baby boy wriggling around in the crib that had been vacant for years, and I lost it. I cried and prayed and called my mama.

The Secret

I have a big mouth. I despise secrets. People asked me *The Question* almost daily. Now I had an actual answer to offer but could not share it. Mark advised us not to tell Houston about the baby until we were ready for the whole world to know. We would tell him closer to the due date. Mark also advised us not to inform friends and family so we would not be tempted to divulge too much of the baby's story, wisely warning that once information is out, it stays out.

When you involve others, they may task you with justifying your decisions. Jeff knew if I told *my* friends too early, I would wear them out by the due date. I hate secrets, but I had to keep this one to protect Houston's peace of mind and the baby's privacy. Plus, Kerri and I actually knew a few of the same people: one of my friends taught Kerri in high school and a church friend's husband was Lynn's doctor. I did not want anyone to say or do anything that could jeopardize placement. So, when I got *The Question* I apologetically lied, "No news." Inside my mind was a cyclone of what-ifs.

Of course, my mama knew, and I did confide in my friend Tobi because we were in the same boat. I shopped weekly at Food City, and eventually even confessed my baby news to our pregnant cashier after she caught me buying diapers. Like I said, I hate secrets. Tobi and I coached and consoled each other via email chats and phone calls for weeks.

Learning, Planning, Praying

At this point in Kerri's and my relationship, all I could do was hope she and the baby were healthy. I had no direct contact with her, so on my end, I sorted through all different types of scenarios, in the form of lists. I bought a pretty notebook and wrote down what to take to the hospital if Jeff and I were allowed to be there. I listed what to send to interim care if the baby went to foster placement in the case Kerri was unsure. I made insurance and medical to-do lists. I made a list of nursery items to buy before he was born (things that could be donated or refunded) and items to buy once we brought him home. I updated my address book and categorized all the friends and family I would have to call or email the moment he was born, the day he came home, and the day Kerri and Bryant's rights were terminated.

When I was pregnant with Houston, my Aunts Judy and Ramona threw me a beautiful baby shower. I shared my baby news and ultrasound pictures with everyone. I shopped for Houston and planned for our hospital stay and the days after. I wrote thank-you notes for gifts from friends and family.

With Kerri's baby, I had only a fifty-fifty chance of needing all those plans, lists, and purchases. I savored my huge secret with restrained enthusiasm.

Another example of my hesitance and worry was the

fact that I could not refer to the baby by name. We planned to name a son Scott after my daddy, but when talking about this child, I simply called him "the baby." Kerri's calling him London was unsettling but understandable. I stuck with "the baby."

February 13, 2010 I wrote.

Dear Baby,

I'll be 36 tomorrow. I started my quest for you in the fall of 2002! Here we are, 7 ½ years later and I feel like you are really close. Kerri's due date is May 21 but she thinks she'll deliver sooner. I cannot tell you how excited I am. I told Grandmama today that we are "paralyzed with thought." Does that make sense? I think about you, Kerri, and Bryant, and how I will tell Houston he has a brother on the way. What a privilege it is to be considered to parent someone else's child. I'm staying ahead in my school work and getting your room ready so that once you are here, we can meet everyone and have fun.

Last week, I met Kerri, her mother, Lauren, and another Bethany intern for lunch at Calhoun's Restaurant. I was terrified someone we know would see us and figure out what was happening. Kerri looks different from my friends: she has flat-ironed, dyed-black hair, and wears dark, tapered skinny jeans. My friends and I worry about hair body and bounce and wear Spanx and mom jeans! One of Daddy's buddies was there, but he didn't catch on. I sat right beside Kerri. She talked ninety miles an hour, but every word fascinated me. I like to talk, too. I felt like, listening to her, I could find out what you may be like, so I paid close attention.

She enjoyed being the center of attention and

asked "What else do you want to know about me?" just before she ordered a rich dessert, which I thought was cute and funny. I tried to memorize every word she said so I could tell Grandmama.

I like Kerri. Really, that's what the whole decision came down to—I feel like I can trust her. I hope I'm right! If I am, Houston will have a baby brother in 11 weeks. Kerri is strong; most girls choose another option. I asked my OB/GYN why so few women choose adoption. She said, "I try to talk to them, but it's like trying to get fish to swim upstream."

Social and familial currents push girls in crisis pregnancies toward abortion or single parenting.

Lauren said you will be born at St. Mary's. That's great because our cousins Dan, Grady, Rosalind, and Oliver were born there, and I know my way around. Also, St. Mary's staff is accustomed to adoption births and should be respectful of our needs and emotions. I don't know if your daddy and I will be there or not; that is up to Kerri. I would love to be in the room when you are delivered but may have to sacrifice that experience.

I arranged another lunch date with Kerri for February 17. I will be alone with Kerri this time so maybe we can talk more openly.

It's hard to comprehend what Kerri is thinking. Daddy and I are nervous and hopeful. Houston has no idea yet; we may wait to tell him until you are born, and the coast is clear. Even if Kerri seems one hundred percent sure before the birth, the possibility remains that she could change her mind, even after you come home with us, until her rights are terminated in court about two weeks later. Whatever the outcome, we are on our way to you, my angel.
Mama

At our lunch I asked Kerri if I could attend her next OB/GYN appointment. To my delight she welcomed me and told me when and where to go. I have terrible spatial reasoning and a poor sense of direction. I was so nervous about the appointment that I rehearsed the drive there.

I printed out MapQuest directions and drove to Dr. T's (I refer to him this way for his privacy) office at St. Mary's the day before. On the appointment day I allowed myself forty-five minutes to make the twenty-minute drive. In the parking garage, I checked my make-up a dozen times, burned a few minutes talking to my mama on the cell phone, and prayerfully braced myself for a bumpy ride. Again, a thought cyclone pounded in my head as I left my car and traversed through the oddly conjoined parking garage, hospital, and towers. I am fairly sure that every time I went to the doctor with Kerri, I traveled a different route.

I was first to the office. I did not know what to do. The clipboard in the small front reception room screamed "Sign In," but why would I? I just sat in the corner. I probably looked like a nut. I felt like an awkward giant. It did not help that I was weighed down with a huge, splitting shopping bag crammed full of maternity clothes I had collected from friends.

This is something to confess: Kerri needed maternity clothes and I knew my generous friends would give me some. To protect my secret, I told my friends the clothes were for Bethany birthmothers but, really, I collected them for Kerri. I did give the larger outfits to the agency so I did not feel too guilty.

Several minutes passed and I, second-guessing myself, left my mound of maternity clothes, walked to the front desk, and asked the receptionist, "Do you have an appointment for Kerri today?"

"Yes" she said, "Are you with her?"

I candidly answered, "Actually, I am adopting her baby, and I would like to meet the doctor."

She reacted with no emotion, "The doctor isn't here today. Kerri is seeing the nurse practitioner. When they call her to come back, just go with her."

I sat back down, disappointed that I would not meet the doctor that day. I surveyed the small room to see pregnant girls, some obviously fifteen or more years younger than I. Pregnant patients, who had heard all I just said, looked at me. I scanned fingers for wedding bands and saw few.

All of my obstetrician appointments during the years of fertility treatments and routine exams were miserable.

This was the first time I had been to an obstetrician with an optimistic attitude. I felt "expectant" in a way but carried the sinking realization that all during the next four months my paper pregnancy held a fifty percent chance of miscarriage.

Kerri and Lynn entered the office right on time. One of Kerri's strong suits is punctuality, which was crucially helpful in soothing my worries. I showed her the clothes, and she laughed at a dorky nightgown my mother had purchased for her. Kerri texted, and Lynn and I talked until a nurse peeked into the waiting room and called, "Kerri?"

The three of us squeezed through a narrow hallway and into a tight little exam room. Trying to stay out of the way, I wedged myself between a plastic cross-section reproductive system and a heavy closet door that refused to latch shut. The nurse practitioner hastily entered the room and gave Kerri instructions.

Kerri, lying flat on her back with ultra-sound gel smeared over her belly, said to the practitioner, "This is Jody."

The woman looked to me and asked, "Who are you, a friend?"

Pointing to her shiny belly, Kerri said, "Jody's going to be his mom."

With a burst of confidence after hearing Kerri's declaration, I stated, "I am adopting the baby from Kerri."

The nurse practitioner congratulated me. She rushed through the exam, helped Kerri up, said "It was nice to meet you Jody," and left.

At the next appointment, I met Dr. T. Kerri and Lynn had told me he was a larger than life character. I really hoped he would be a normal, down-to-earth person with whom I could communicate academically and look to for guidance and help through the pregnancy and delivery in May.

No such luck. Dr. T is a great guy and a wonderful doctor, but he is not plain or predictable. At seemingly seven feet tall, he absorbed every inch of what was left of the tiny exam room, and his intimidating stature and booming voice pushed me closer to the plastic uterus. I stood in the corner again holding that stubborn closet door closed.

Dr. T loudly asked, "Well, who is this here?"

Kerri, again said, "Jody. She's going to be his mom. She's adopting my baby."

Dr. T looked at me. "Wonderful. I heard that was the plan. It's a pleasure to meet you, Jody."

I told him I had looked forward to meeting him because Kerri and Lynn just adored him.

Lynn boasted, "Dr. T is an opera singer!"

Dr. T explained that he sings with an opera group that performs annually at Carnegie Hall in New York City.

Say what?

I expected a doctor with a calm bedside manner. This guy was a wild man loudly spinning opera tales, jokes, and literary references. His personality served as a diversion from the stress. I liked him, but I had hoped for someone simple, typical, and reassuring.

When the appointment ended, he looked at me and boomed, "Well, Jody, it was a true pleasure to meet you. I want you to know that you are welcome in my delivery room or operating room any time, and that you should wear that color blue often. It looks stunning with your eyes."

I half expected him to tap dance backward out of the room waving jazz hands. He was bigger than life, and so was my situation. I went to more appointments where Dr. T loudly performed. He won me over by always greeting me and showing me respect. He always acted like he had no doubt I would be Kerri's baby's mother. He was not who I expected, or who I thought I wanted, but I liked him because, as I said before, I am attracted to characters. Many weeks later Dr. T turned out to be exactly who Kerri *and* I needed.

Surviving The Wait

But they that wait upon the LORD
shall renew their strength;
they shall mount up with wings as eagles;
they shall run, and not be weary;
and they shall walk, and not faint.

—Isaiah 40:31

I played clarinet in The University of Tennessee Marching Band. Often, as soldiers say, we hurried up to wait. The UT Band marched in Clinton's inaugural parade, and we stood outside freezing for four hours near the Smithsonian Mall before our turn to step off. That was nothing. The nine months of pregnancy with Houston were a breeze compared to the slow, cautious, profound wait I endured with Kerri.

During the first month after Jeff and I met Kerri, I did my best not to the think about the baby. Shakespeare writes in *Macbeth*:

Life's but a walking shadow, a poor player
That struts and frets his hour upon the stage

~ 128 ~

And then is heard no more. It is a tale
Told by an idiot, full of sound and fury,
Signifying nothing.

I often speculated, *am I a poor player on the* adoption *stage, fretting my days away toward a baby or toward nothing?* I did not dare fantasize about swaddling Kerri's baby in a flannel blanket, lathering him with Johnson's bedtime soap in the "Whale of a Tub," strolling him around during Houston's Knox Sox baseball games, or showing him off to my friends. When my mind wandered in that direction, I did one of the following: I wrote in my journal, fine-tuned my lists, prayed for Kerri, bought Kerri a treat, or cranked up my kitchen radio and sipped wine.

Coping with such an incomprehensible wait proved to be one of the greatest challenges of my life. My prayers became unceasing. I held a continuous conversation with God. Remember, the only folks on my end who knew about this baby were my mother, my friend Tobi, and the pregnant Food City cashier.

I bought a huge wicker basket to store all of the symbols of my neurosis, in other words, Kerri's gifts. I went to bed at 8:00 p.m. to make the days go by faster. I love Pinot Grigio, but, as I was saving for an adoption placement fee, raising Houston, taking college courses, and filling Kerri's basket dollar by dollar, I made the switch to economical boxed wine for my kitchen radio relaxation routine! Toby Keith, you may be friends with "Red Solo Cup," but Bota Box became one of my BFFs!

Life Goes On Outside My Head

As I fretted my days away, I aimed to get to know Kerri better. My purpose was two-fold. First, Bethany counselors repeatedly told waiting mothers that when linked with a birthparent, a ministerial, service-oriented attitude would quiet worries. Honored to know a young woman so courageous, I felt compelled to serve Kerri, mentor her, and be her friend. My second purpose in getting to know Kerri was to continually assess my risk. Though I had no control over her, and she absolutely could change her mind at any second, when I was with Kerri, I could read her and surmise the likelihood of her following through with placement. As I secretly "dated" my hopeful future son's birthmother, the rest of the world carried on. I wrote to the baby in late February.

> *Dear Baby,*
> *It is cold and gloomy outside today. I really need the sun to come out. You are a perfect ray of light coming in the spring! You will bring so much joy to our home, our families, and our friends! I can't wait to meet Kerri again this Friday for lunch to learn more about you.*
> *Love,*
> *Mama*

I was feeling closer to Kerri. My confidence grew with our familiarity. Exhausted from thinking and worrying that day, I resolved to live the experience full-force and "go for broke."

I decided to savor each soaring summit and tumbling trench I encountered. If my heart was broken, it would heal. That was the first time in my journal I confirmed belief that Kerri's baby would be *my* son. I started shopping for my baby boy, due in May.

Shaken Not Stirred

Just stand out there
and stick your glove out in the air.
I'll take care of it.

—"Benny" in *The Sandlot*

The adoption journey worked me over like a Smoky Mountain potter would a fat wad of gray wet clay. I am still me but I am tempered, more colorful, kilned. Kerri loves tattoos and piercings. I like costume jewelry. She listens to loud, head-banging alternative bands. I listen mostly to country music. She watches wrestling. I watch Houston's baseball and basketball games. Kerri hated school. I am a teacher. She has a rat. I have a Yorkie.

Kerri has taught me a great deal about humanity, humility, and most of all, patience. Kerri, like many in her generation, prefers texting to email and talking on the phone, so I had to adapt. I have a rinky-dink flip phone so I am slow, but I can type with one finger like a mad man now. Kerri taught me to text!

In March, when she was about thirty-four weeks pregnant, Kerri had some false labor and panicked because she could not get in touch with me. Lynn asked if we could exchange phone numbers, just in case. I fearfully agreed, not really knowing the right choice. I am glad I did. From then on, whenever I felt apprehensive, I texted Kerri. She always promptly texted back. Often during Houston's ballgames, I secretly texted Kerri. At the time only Kerri, Jeff, my mother, Tobi, the cashier, and I knew about Scotty. As Charlton Heston as Moses said in The Ten Commandments movie, "let it be written" that I can indeed keep a secret.

During our many lunches together, I observed Kerri graciously respond to trite pregnancy questions asked by unknowing waiters. I listened in awe as she introduced me as Scotty's soon to be mother. I watched her expertly dodge strife with her mother and family members. I think in circles and darts, as I tell my students, but I try to keep the darts from flying. Because of the lessons I learned from Kerri and adoption, I try to be a kinder, more forgiving person. While getting to know Kerri, I became less inhibited and, honestly, more myself. I learned that other people can help me and I should ask for help sometimes. I talk more openly about my faith and take chances with my sense of humor. And, I learned the importance of thinking before speaking. As I spent time with Kerri and her mother, I habitually crafted every word that left my mouth. I tried not to hurt their feelings and to always show acceptance and compassion. Many times, Kerri or Lynn asked me a question and I prayed in my mind, *God, please make the right words come out of my mouth so I do not offend them and they do not doubt their plan for the baby.*

Another tense moment occurred while Kerri, Lynn, and I had lunch one day. Kerri told me her plan to move back up North after the baby was born. Lynn asked, "Jody, is there any way, after Kerri moves, I can see London? I just want to see what he looks like and see that he's okay."

I silently prayed. I sucked it up, and I answered "Lynn, I don't see any reason why you and I can't meet one day so you can hold him and see what he's like, as long as that's fine with Kerri."

Lynn slid out of her side of the booth and embraced me, sobbing, "Thank you. Thank you. Thank you. You don't know what that means to me. This is my first grandchild, and I love him so much."

Grandchild. Whoa!

The summer before I met Kerri, a friend of mine approached me at a baseball game. She asked me how the adoption wait was going. We talked about adoption a few minutes and she confided in me that she became pregnant in college and placed the baby for adoption. She explained that only her immediate family knew.

In awe of her strength and willingness to open up to me, I asked, "What should I do when I meet birthparents and possibly get to know them before the birth?"

She advised, "Keep reassuring them that you and Jeff will be great parents. Also, do your best to understand that birthparents aren't the only ones giving up this baby. Their families will suffer and may be furious."

I followed her advice and made sure to form a positive relationship with Lynn and with Kerri's friends. The nature of our relationship naturally evolved toward open adoption. I tried to set realistic expectations for their future with the baby, but this was my first rodeo, so I made mistakes. My motto was to *Err on the side of kindness*. Mark and Terri told me God takes care of the details. I figured if my motivations were pure, God would fix my greenhorn bloopers.

Speaking of bloopers, the more I learned, the more I laughed. The more I laughed, the more I realized that when God said to me, "She is on her way," He meant Kerri.

I wrote to the baby in April, five weeks before the due date.

Dear Scotty,

This is the first time I've written to you using your name. I've been afraid. Mark says any situation is 50/50 and I should be excited but brace myself. I hope my relationships with Kerri, Bryant, and Lynn help them see the plan through. I concentrate mostly on being a friend to Kerri. She fascinates me. She asked Daddy and me if we had told Houston about you yet. I had to answer very carefully because I didn't want her to think I didn't trust her. I told Kerri the truth; we had not told Houston, because if we involved Houston at this point, he would be over the moon and if she changed her mind, he would be devastated. She handled it well and assured me she would not change her mind. I have to protect Houston as long as possible. He will love you so much and badly wants a brother. I try not to think about you too much because I get so nervous and afraid Kerri will keep you. I talked to Bryant for about an hour recently. He is smart and funny, just like he wrote on his Bethany paperwork.

Daddy and I had lunch with Kerri and Lynn yesterday at El Chico's on Merchants Drive. It was a beautiful spring day (April 14) so we sat on the patio. I felt at peace, hopeful, and happy to be with them. Lynn is having a hard time thinking of letting you go. I brought her a photo album. It was zebra print with green binding (not a baby theme). I said it suited her because she's a wild woman! Lynn is full of personality and eagerly showed us her tattoos! Your frat-boy Presbyterian daddy was quite amused. See you soon!
Love,
Mama

As Kerri, Lynn, and I became closer, they divulged more family facts that surprised and challenged me.

Lynn told me that she was in a stuntwoman group in high school. She performed in local commercials and once even donned a gorilla suit. She said in her biggest stunt she jumped off the top of a furniture store roof onto a stack of mattresses. Knoxville is a cinema town with lots of production companies, but even so, this was some wild news.

It got stranger. Once, after a lunch at The Original Louis' on Old Broadway in Knoxville, Lynn begged me to visit the bird store nearby where she "bought all Tanner's food and got his wings clipped" — not a conversation I had ever had in my life. Tanner the parrot lives in a mammoth cage in Lynn's living room. We visited the store, and I saw birds I did not know existed, especially in Knoxville, Tennessee. Lynn was so excited to show me Tanner. She invited me to come to Kerri's and her home to meet him in person.

That was certainly a time when I prayed silently about what decision to make. I did not want to set an uncomfortable precedent, and I did not want to appear snobby. I prayed that God would guide my choice and words. I went.

Kerri rode with me in my car, another source of stress. I drive an old GMC Jimmy I call Big Red. Well, Big Red has seen better days and parts of her are loud and ugly. She grunts up hills, and I must roll my window halfway down and grasp the glass to close my door or else the interior plastic and leather panel will pull away from the frame. Luckily, Big Red was clean and I had parked on a slope so I could inconspicuously close the door.

I thought, *Be a safe driver Jody. Don't have a fender bender with Scotty's birthmother in the car. That would be horrible. She probably would cancel the deal.* Kerri hopped in and said, "I like your truck." God handles the details.

The five-minute drive felt like twenty as I white-knuckle gripped the steering wheel and employed intense peripheral vision to be a super-defensive driver. We arrived without injury.

The moment I entered Lynn's front door, Tanner the parrot squawked, "Hello" but not just any "Hello." He spoke in a hillbilly accent!

I met the rat, too. Kerri showed me her room decorated with *Twilight, Transformers,* and *Alice in Wonderland* posters. I looked at her dresser mirror and was startled to see pictures of Houston, Jeff and me taped to the glass. I had given Kerri some originals from the profile to show her friends. At that moment I was convinced her baby was truly our Scotty.

But then I looked into Lynn's room. There stood a fully assembled Pack-N-Play. The navy and beige plaid portable crib stood ready for a napping baby at the edge of Lynn's bed. Shaken, I managed my way down the hall to the kitchen, only to see a string of ultrasound photos stuck to the refrigerator.

Why?

I managed to calmly talk through the remaining time with them. As I left, the West African bird with the Appalachian accent screeched a farewell "Bah- bah!"

On my way home, the cyclone stirred once more. *Why does Lynn have a Pack-N-Play? And why do they want to look at those ultrasound pictures every day?*

For I know the thoughts that I think toward you,
saith the LORD,
thoughts of peace, and not of evil,
to give you an expected end.

—Jeremiah 29:11

Comparing and Contrasting (Not Contracting)

I think the pregnancy journey is lived week to week. I tracked Houston's development through doctor visits and websites like storknet.com and babycenter.com. I recall Houston's movement in my abdomen and how I relished watching my tummy bounce with his hiccups. In contrast, I lived the adoption journey moment to moment, primarily in secret, mostly in my mind. When pregnant, I felt and saw progress toward my goal of a healthy baby. With adoption, I measured progress by sporadic meetings with Dr. T, who breathed noise, humor, and life into the stressful appointments. I was also comforted by updates from Bethany counselors, and numerous texts and visits with Kerri and her family.

I loved placing my hand on my stomach and feeling Houston kick and roll. The first time I laid my hand on Kerri's tummy and felt Scotty kick, I was overcome with humility and emotion. Kerri was so free with me. I was so restrained. I did not know how to react. It was challenging to comprehend that I would raise the baby who grew inside her. I became attached to Scotty and Kerri and the stakes grew higher.

I called Bryant. I told him Lynn had a Pack-N-Play in her bedroom. When we spoke, I found him to be articulate and blunt. He said that members of Kerri's family were against the adoption plan, and I should do my best to make them see I would be a good mother to "London."

He said, "Jody, Kerri really needs you right now. "Some people are fighting her on this. I am doing everything I can to support her, but you are probably the nicest person she has in her life right now. Just keep being there for her, and I'll do everything I can from here."

I want readers to know that I cared for Kerri's family. I sympathized with them. I mean no disrespect to them when I say they were fighting the adoption plan. As a mother, I suspect that if Houston were twenty-one and his girlfriend were pregnant, I would fight adoption, too. I would likely beg him to let me raise the baby if he and his girlfriend could not. As a mother, I identified with Kerri *and* Lynn.

Some days later, before a Waiting Families group meeting, Lauren brought me into Mark's office to talk about how things were going. They coached me on dealing with my recent highs and lows. On a lighter side, I asked, "Am I on Adoption Candid Camera?"

They promised not, and quizzed me. I responded with the abstract, amusing details in Kerri's and my developing relationship and remarked, "I think when this is all over, I'll write a musical comedy for Broadway; I have all the elements: romance, drama, conflict, love and loss, a seven-foot tall opera singing obstetrician, a stunt-woman birth-grandmother, and a pricey West African Grey Parrot with a country twang!"

It's the Southern Way;
when things get too painful,
we either avoid them or we laugh.

—Pat Conroy, *The Prince of Tides*

Anticipatory Grief

Bryant told me Kerri needed me. I do not know if Bryant realized the need for comfort was mutual. Adoption is grief in reverse. I left the dark world of infertility and moved toward the light-filled hope of adoption. Kerri, though, was anticipating grief. I truly believed she was helping me through the burdensome wait and it would be my job to help Bethany counselors lead her out of the darkness.

There was so much more to this than just a baby. As someone who had been pregnant, I related well to some of Kerri's physical and hormonal struggles, but our journeys were quite different. I handled *The Question* carefully, concealing my baby on the way. Kerri, however, could hide nothing. I could take breaks from my struggle because no one knew, while Kerri answered clichéd questions every day. She got no breaks. People noticed her pregnant belly and said to her, "Congratulations! When are you due?" followed by "Is it a boy or a girl?" followed by "What are you going to name him?" followed by "How are you decorating his nursery?" *The Question* paled in comparison to the weight and frequency of inquiries Kerri faced.

Since I had decided to "go for broke" I took risks. I was a month away from Kerri's due date. Scotty was still top secret, so I had to be crafty. My mother bought me a stroller-car-seat combo. She is a retired teacher and I was back in school, so we went to Target, and we picked the cheapest combo that was not pink, not blue, but gender neutral—just in case.

Here is another example of pregnancy versus adoption. If I had been pregnant, I would have assembled the stroller and thrown the box away. Since my adopted baby's coming home was fifty-fifty, an inescapable mortifying fact, I taped the receipt to the box and slid it into the bedroom closet to wait with the "Whale of a Tub," Houston's old but freshly cleaned baby blankets, and my emergency stash of Pampers, wipes, and Similac.

My mother and I took a huge risk of exposing the secret. With thousands of others, we went to the Duck-Duck Goose consignment sale to stock up on baby clothes. We concocted a story to explain our being there in case we were spotted. Luckily, we had a fabulously dramatic and true story to do just the job.

Just weeks before, an old friend of mine, in agonizing pelvic pain, called her mother for help. Suspecting diverticulitis or appendicitis, they hurried to the hospital where an emergency room physician performed an ultra-sound and informed my friend that she was in labor. My friend had no idea she was pregnant. I know there is a show on TV about it, and I know people think those women are idiots, but I saw my friend, who was *not* fat, three weeks before she gave birth and I could not tell. Thankfully, the baby was healthy.

This was a hilariously delicious morsel of gossip but it was extremely tough for me to swallow. Here I was, working my tail off to reassure Kerri and pray my baby into my home, and this woman just popped out a little boy. My friend only "waited" a few hours for her son.

What are the odds that I, someone who had been trying and waiting for *eight* years (almost three thousand days), would actually know one of those women who was pregnant and did not know it?

My friend is a terrific mother. Her baby, who is adored by all who know him, was the perfect diversionary story. *Oh, hey there, we are just buying clothes for my friend who was pregnant and did not know it!*

We stood outside Duck-Duck Goose in line for one hour, paranoid and on high alert, before doors opened. Once we entered, Mama and I raced our way through aisles of baby blue, snatching up newborn to twenty-four month sized outfits. I watched in envy as confident expectant mothers peacefully browsed. Tobi had poignantly noted that when she bought clothes for the Food City baby, she felt like she was "shopping for a ghost." We rushed through the huge event only to end up in a three-hour waiting line to check out.

Of course, a fellow church member landed right behind me in line. I could not dodge this one because I had a cart filled with infant outfits. The diversionary story about my old friend worked fabulously. When I got home, I laid out all the clothes on the full sized bed in Scotty's room. I took pictures of the colorful array of cute outfits to show Kerri. I also ordered a onesie that read "Worth the Wait." I took it to our next obstetrician appointment. To my delight, Kerri said, "That is the cutest thing I've ever seen!" *Whew!* I boldly took such steps in front of her to demonstrate my trust and certainty that she would follow through on the adoption plan. I was trying to convince myself, too.

Be Real, Be Bold

During one lunch, really close to the due date, I asked
Kerri, "Do you see me as this baby's mother?"
She answered, "Yes, I really do."
I then asked, "What is the plan for the hospital?" I was
hoping she wanted me there.
"When I go into labor, I will call you, and you and Jeff
will come to the hospital and hang out until the baby's born,"
Kerri said.
I was overjoyed. I wanted to be there but I did not want
to be pushy. Kerri saying "Of course you guys will be there!
You're his parents!" put me at so much ease.
I explained to Kerri that I wanted to pack a diaper bag
with everything that Scotty would need at the hospital. "You
just pack what you need for you, Kerri, and once he's born, I
will be his mama immediately in every way. I will be there to
take care of Scotty and you. What do you think?" Like I said, I
was going for broke.
"That sounds good, because I'll probably be in lots of
pain," Kerri responded.
I wondered whether she meant physical or emotional.
Kerri demonstrated intent to follow through all along.
She picked up little things at yard sales for Scotty. Her
grandfather bought her a Winnie-the-Pooh bedding set, and she
gave it to me. I had met him once and he was very nice—I did

not know at the time that her grandfather was unsupportive of the adoption plan. When we were together, Kerri and I seemed sure of things. When we were apart, she confronted opposition and hard questions, and I battled isolation and lack of control over my open-ended story.

Bryant

Kerri's social worker Lauren called me February 12 to inform me that Bryant signed the documents to waive his rights. My new friend Bryant stayed true north to Kerri and to me and to the plan for their baby. April 26, 2010, I emailed Bryant.

Hey Bryant! I hope you had a great 21ˢᵗ birthday. I also hope the next day wasn't too rough! Ha! I have filled a basket full of treats for Kerri and thought you'd like to know what's in it. I got her playing cards, an Edward Twilight t-shirt, a handbag, butterfly earrings, lotion, a soft throw blanket, Twix, Hershey bars, Kit Kats, Pizza Pringles, photo albums, Bridget Jones Diary DVDs, a London telephone booth piggy bank (from Houston), pink flip-flops, warm socks, and three Tudor novels. Jeff and I hope to meet you, but we understand if you can't get down here. Thanks for all the tips on what to get her and how to help her. I think so much of Kerri.

Bryant wrote back.

Sounds fantastic, Jody. She's gonna love it and I really hope I can get there.

I sent Bryant a care-package full of funny surprises (a few things about North vs. South and Tennessee—not his favorite state). I also mailed Bryant pictures of Scotty's room, our family, and a pregnant Kerri.

Big News at Baskin-Robbins

Kerri was quickly approaching her May 21 due date when Dr. T decided to induce her labor on May 13, out of respect for Kerri's emotional state and all of the people involved in the birth plan. Dr. T had no idea that May 13 was also Jeff's birthday. Kerri, antsy about having everything planned out, texted me one night in late April and asked if Houston knew yet. She typed something along the lines of "I really want you and Jeff to go ahead and tell Houston about the baby. I know I won't back out."

She also said she wanted to finally meet Houston. I remember I was sitting in my rocking chair, watching TV, and contemplating just how to introduce them and tell Houston he would have a brother in two weeks. I thought, *Show her you trust her. Risk everything so she trusts you.*

I texted Kerri back, "Why don't *you* tell Houston about the baby?"

She replied, "That would be awesome! Are you sure?"

"Yes, I am sure."

We planned to meet at Baskin Robbins at 3:00 p.m. on Thursday, April 29, fourteen days before the due date, where we would have ice cream and Kerri would tell Houston the big news!

Thursday afternoon I left my last class at Pellissippi

State Community College in a hurry and drove straight to Sequoyah Elementary to check Houston out. It was about 2:25 p.m., and I had to pull Houston from school early to get to Kerri on time. I signed the checkout book and asked the school secretary to call for Houston. The secretary said, "I'm sorry honey, we can't check students out after 2:15. It's a new rule."

"Well, I really need him. This is important."

She insisted, "Well, you'll have to wait until school is out because I can't call him."

"Please, this is a family situation. He has to come with me now."

She kept touting the rule, in place because too many parents checked their kids out just before the bell, and it made dismissal chaotic.

I finally demanded, "Either you call him or I'm going down there to get him. I will tell you tomorrow why he is leaving, but trust me; you will be very upset with yourself if you don't let him leave now."

That did the trick. I was not about to let her be the fourth person to find out about Scotty, and I certainly was not going to allow her to make us late.

Once Houston was buckled into the backseat, I told him we were going to meet some friends for ice cream. He asked, "Who are they?" Operating on the fly, I just told him their names.

When we got to Baskin Robbins, I introduced Kerri and Lynn to Houston, and we all ordered our ice creams. Kerri was visibly tense. I said, "Are you okay? Are you ready to tell Houston? Once you tell him, Kerri, there is no going back."

"I am nervous," Kerri said, "but I am ready."

After small talking for a while, Lynn excused herself so I walked outside with her and gave Kerri the nod. Houston's freckled face and big blue eyes looked to me for explanation as I left the booth. Lynn and I chatted a few minutes and Kerri came to the door and said we could come back in.

"Houston, what do you think?"

He said he was happy. While he digested Superman sherbet and the exciting announcement, he appeared generally calm, kind, and polite, but I could tell his eight-year-old mind was struggling to comprehend Kerri's news.

Twenty or so minutes later Houston hopped out of the booth and said, "I'm ready to go." As is his obnoxious habit, he took off out the door onto the sidewalk. I made a few weak excuses about his behavior, worried that I looked like a bad parent because he was not completely obedient. Kerri was sweet and did not seem to think he was too wild. In the car on the way home I said, "Now that we are alone, tell me how you really feel." He answered with a dramatic exhale.

"Overwhelmed."

Friday, April 30, I emailed Bryant.

Bryant, I was so proud of Keri yesterday. She and Houston were shy at first, but I think they got along well. Houston said he thinks Kerri is sweet. He was shocked by the news, but now he is getting excited about having a brother! I think, because he's waited so long, the news was hard to believe. He was looking forward to telling his teacher about the baby this morning. You are giving him something I cannot give him. Jeff and I think so much of you and Kerri.

Bryant replied.

I'm glad they got along so well, and he's happy about it. Kerri told me Houston said he would look out for the baby, which is amazing and everything I'd want for him. Just in the short time we've spoken and known each other, there's no doubt in my mind that you and your family are very deserving of this and I'm glad that Kerri and I can give you this opportunity since we can't do it and all. Kerri's getting to the impatient stage where she just wants him out. The big guy is causing havoc in her womb. LOL.

That day at school, Houston's teacher, Mrs. Robinson, allowed him to gleefully announce his big news to the whole class. Teachers, buddies, and Principal Hill congratulated him. Houston's attitude changed from "overwhelmed" and quiet to eager and talkative once he told his friends about Scotty. I suppose the baby brother on the way seemed more real to Houston once Houston's peers knew.

I told Mark that Houston knew and he said, "Here we go! Now you can tell the world!"

I called my Uncle Dan with the big news. He could not believe my mother and I kept such a huge secret.

I completed my teacher certification courses May 8. At our last class, I told my intuitive friend Karen that she had been right a few months before when she had predicted I would get my baby once all our coursework was finished. She, too, was impressed by my self-control in secret-keeping. Since we often carpooled to class, I was proud that I had spared her my worrisome thoughts!

When I told my buddy Amber she exclaimed, "Jody, oh my gosh! I don't think I can make it! How am I going to make it?"

I laughed, "I'll help you get through this!"

I called Stevens and said, "Go to Kroger, buy two pounds of ground beef, make my casserole, freeze it, and bring it over here in two weeks!"

My wonderful friends buoyed me as I tread water for those two weeks.

My friends and family demonstrated confidence, but doubt remained.

I went to dinner with a few girlfriends one night. I did not know one of the ladies, but all had informed her of my pending baby. She politely congratulated me but immediately likened my situation to that of her friend, who welcomed a baby home and cared deeply for him only to greet a social worker at the door a few days later. That child's birthmother changed her mind, and the social worker had to take the baby back. Many such stories began with confident, committed birthparents. I heard her say the word "nightmare." I guess she was just trying to considerately warn me, as if I were unaware of the risks.

The Hospital

I asked Mark, "How do we handle the hospital situation? I am a wreck. What should Jeff and I do all day?" Mark stressed that we should simply take care of Kerri and do whatever she needed us to do.

"You are possibly the closest thing Kerri has ever known to Jesus," Mark assured us.

I questioned, "Huh? So, I've completed two years of paperwork, an eighty-two item to do list, gotten a Rabies shot for Buzz, and now I have to be Jesus?"

We had a good laugh over that, and Mark primed us for what types of things can go on in adoption cases in the hospital.

When pregnant with Houston, I read *What to Expect When You Are Expecting*. No such book exists for adoption because there is no predictability, no concrete truth, and no typical path. There are plenty of books and resources covering adoption-related topics but adoption is a dynamic, evolving industry. Mark advised Jeff and me well, but there is no way to be completely prepared for "the hospital experience."

I told Houston that he may get to come to the hospital to see his baby brother. Houston said, "Mama, I don't think that's a good idea. If Kerri sees how cute I am, she may think about how cute Scotty is going to be and want to keep him."

We all were afraid. I ate lunch with Houston at school on Wednesday, May 12 and ran into many friends who cheered us on.

That afternoon, I did another test-drive to the St. Mary's Women's Pavilion, where Scotty would be born the next day. I introduced myself to the receptionist and explained the situation. She was sweet and promised to give me the elevator code to the labor and delivery floor the following morning. Houston sang in the children's choir at church that evening, and again, my buddies were curious, anxious, and encouraging about the next day, Delivery Day!

By now everyone knew about Scotty. Karen, our associate pastor's wife, asked "What time do you want Mark [her husband] to come see you at St. Mary's?"

I sadly explained that no one could come. Even the best adoption hospital situations are stressful and tenuous. Even if our plans were set and strong, any change in arrangements or any additional visitors could affect the outcome.

My friend Amber asked me again how she and our friends would survive the next few days. I said, "Well, Amber, I am there for you!"

My friend Rita reached out to me in an email at 12:17 a.m. on Thursday, May 13, 2010.

Hi Jody,
It is officially May 13th, and you are on my mind and in my prayers. The Lord will guide you all through the next hours. I am praying for an easy delivery, and for everything we talked about at school today. I told my parents what Houston said about going to the hospital. My dad was awestruck by the depth of his thinking and concern. You have a wonderful son and God is bringing you another one to raise up in the way he should go.
I love ya,
Rita

I wrote back.

Rita,

You made me cry. I feel prepared to face whatever comes today. Through this "journey" I have found tremendous strength in God as a Heavenly Father. I have also found that I have loyal, genuine, incredibly kind friends. You have no idea how often I have been really worried and you have magically appeared! I love you. Stay tuned....

Go Time

A boy's story is the best that is ever told.

—Charles Dickens

The Dyers' "hospital plan" was in place. While Jeff and I survived St. Mary's, my mother would care for Houston at our house. With my lists, overnight bag, and diaper bag stuffed and in the car, I drove Houston to school.

While in the car line, I watched little children bearing lumpy backpacks trot into the building, and I thought to myself, *What a burden I am carrying today that could become a blessing like no other. All these children and parents are starting a simple, normal day and I am about to experience something momentous.* I told Houston I loved him as he hopped out of the car. He seemed un-phased by the magnitude of the day and was probably just as excited about school almost being out for summer and his Grandmama spending the night.

I pulled away from his school and slowly turned left to follow the car line uphill. A couple of cars ahead of me, I saw my friend Michael's hand reach out the window and he, knowing exactly where I was headed, gave me a strong, spirited fist pump.

I drove out of my neighborhood of support and headed northeast toward the hospital.

Just as I had practiced the afternoon before, I parked in the garage. I left my overnight bag and the diaper bag in the car. This had been Jeff's suggestion, since we did not know if we would be allowed to spend the night and did not want to appear forceful. Jeff and Mark met me in the lobby. Mark advised us to just "hang out" and "find some place to be" and not stay in Kerri's room too much, just periodically check on her.

To Jeff's dismay and embarrassment, I introduced myself to the nursing staff and explained who I was, why I was there, and then said, "I will be Scotty's mother. Kerri and I have a close relationship, and she understands that I will be his mother the moment he is born. Any questions about pediatrics, testing, and appointments should come to me. Please know that I will be doing everything I can to help Kerri. I know you often have adoption cases, but ours is very open."

They were polite and welcoming, but appeared a little shocked at my boldness. They gave me a hospital bracelet, a plastic band with a metal clip and typed words linking Kerri, our soon-to-be-born son, and me.

When I first walked into Kerri's hospital room, she exclaimed, "I weigh 155 pounds!"

She enjoyed a good chuckle when I said, "I do, too!"

Nurses performed the routine procedures to induce Kerri's labor, but progress was extremely slow. Jeff and I roamed the hospital, checked on Kerri, talked with Lynn and Kerri's friends, and kept out of the way. Mostly, we sat and stared at each other in the first floor waiting room, two levels down from Kerri. I asked a thousand times, "What do you think we should do?" and Jeff answered a thousand times, "Just sit here."

Kerri's birthparent counselor Lauren was out of town for her sister's wedding, so Kerri and I leaned on Mark, agency director Terri, and each other for care. I could tell that Lauren did an incredible job preparing Kerri for her time in the hospital.

We passed the time as best we could. Kerri enjoyed looking through her big basket of goodies. She and her friends played cards. As they played, I scrutinized the fetal monitor. I relied strictly on Kerri's cues and the hospital room's equipment for a sense of progress; I could not feel any contractions and I got little information from doctors or nurses. When in Kerri's room, I tried to listen to and focus on Kerri, but the fetal monitor screen beeped and flashed for my attention. Sporadically, a nurse included me by asking me a question. My favorite was, "Mrs. Dyer, are you going to breastfeed?"

I laughed, "I probably look like I can, but no."

Most of the nurses, especially Lisa and Jane, treated me like the baby's mother and Kerri's friend, and I appreciated it. I still felt awkward unless I was with Kerri. All of those lunches we had shared paid off. Our relationship saved my sanity.

As I meandered the labor and delivery unit, I envied pregnant women who, barring rare tragedy, had a one hundred percent chance of taking their babies home. *Fifty-fifty* pounded in my head. Family and friends texted me like clockwork with cheering messages. Paige routinely asked, "What's going on?" to which I replied so many times, "Just waiting." I could not talk on the phone much because Lynn, Kerri, Mark and Terri, or Kerri's friends were usually with me.

Days earlier, I created a huge email contact group and gave my log in and password to my friend Jamie, who volunteered to relay messages. I had no computer access. Waiting parents, if you go to the hospital, take a laptop so you can communicate with the outside world. Jamie also gave me a bottle of champagne and an Ambien. My friends understood my frailties and respected the raw, unknown elements of the hospital experience.

Our goal was vaginal delivery by 5:00 p.m. but that did not happen. Kerri did not dilate as needed, so Dr. T decided to perform a Cesarean section. Kerri panicked. Her plan was way off track, and she was terrified of the operation. I panicked, too. Usually, the baby stays in the hospital until the birthmother is released. With a vaginal delivery, Kerri probably would go home on Saturday. After a C-section, they could keep her until Monday.

For a normal mother-to-be, that is a painful inconvenience. For me, it was a potential nightmare and left room for the birth family to bond with Scotty, question Kerri's decisions, and break the promise and our hearts. Concealing my self-involved panic, I reassured Kerri that she would be fine. "It's almost over. I love you, and I am proud of you," I said. Jeff gave Kerri a fatherly kiss on top of her head just before nurses rolled her into the operating room.

By this time, several more of Kerri's family members had arrived. Out of respect for their suffering, Jeff and I did not go into the family waiting room, but Kerri wanted Jeff and me to be the first to see Scotty, so we needed to stay close by.

I asked the nurses where we should wait, and one hastily replied, "Just go into Room 32, but please don't touch anything." That crushing comment reminded me of how fragile my position as "mother" really was.

When I delivered Houston, a dozen or so family members joyfully waited at the hospital. After he was born, they fought for position at the nursery window to watch nurses scrub him down and hold him up for all to see. No one came to the hospital to await Scotty's arrival, per our request at the advice of Bethany social workers.

Family and friends on "our side" could jeopardize placement by demonstrating ownership, saying the wrong thing, appearing over-confident, etc. Mark advised, "The fewer the people there, the better." He was right. I was in no condition to console a worried relative.

I called Jamie so she could update my friends. Jamie alerted.

> *Hey girls! I am just waiting to hear from Jody. Kerri dilated only 5cm, so the doctor decided to do a C-section. This was about 6:15 p.m. Jody is nervous, but positive. I will let you know when I hear from Jody. Say a prayer for all.*
> *Jamie*

He Is Here!

An eternity passed. Jeff and I held our breath. We did not speak for about thirty minutes. Jeff pitched forward and swayed backward in the hardwood rocker facing me. I sat tensely on the slick edge of the room's hospital blue plastic-skinned loveseat, straining to find any audible clue to relieve my stress: the opening of a double door, nurses' chatter, gurney wheels, Kerri's voice.

Envision the scene. Room 32 held a kind social worker and a tired couple, who had tried to get pregnant, then adopt, for a total of eight years. They were minutes away from the delivery of a dream. They prayed. They waited. Down the hall, in a sterile operating room, a dramatic doctor, a grandmother on the cusp of saying goodbye to her first grandchild, and a petite heroine toiled to bring that dream into the world. Between those two rooms, a loud, agitated, grieving family flooded and filled a barren waiting room.

After an impossible wait, noise finally leaked under the door to Room 32. I stood and walked to the door. I gently opened the door to sneak a look into the hall, and met Lynn face to face. She proclaimed, "He's here, and he's beautiful."

Scotty was born at 7:21 p.m. I rushed into the hall ahead of Mark and Jeff to see him. Jeff cautioned. I argued.

Mark used his social worker intuition to keep things smooth. He coached, "Jody, wait."

"But Kerri wants us to see him first."

"Let's give her family a little time."

I watched, like a spectator, a red-shirted athlete on the sidelines not allowed to touch the ball. Led by Lynn, a blur of metal rails, white sheets, uniforms, and Kerri's microburst of a family blew by without a single gesture in our direction.

I watched them roll away. In the center of the mob, I spotted Kerri, tucked and covered in white blankets. She cradled a tiny package. Finally, as they neared Kerri's room, the whirlwind died down and broke apart.

I saw my son for the first time, in his mother's arms.

He and I were completely, mutually vulnerable in that moment. I looked directly into his puffy face, into his glossy eyes, and, recognized, *There he is.*

I wanted to grab him and go home. He was born. Alive. *Real.* He was no longer eight hard years away. He was twenty feet down the hall. Even so, he still evaded me. I had no power.

Reality in the Raw

I knew he was my son, but I had no control, no cemented authority over him. *Fifty-fifty*. Kerri's family poured like a tidal wave into her room. They surrounded her with noise and emotion. Several minutes later, Dr. T strolled down to Kerri's room. When he saw the commotion, he came to Kerri's and my rescue. He was close to Kerri and thus aware of her physical pain and emotional anxiety. Protecting Kerri's welfare and aiming to respect her original birthing plan, Dr. T put his status and stature into action. He loudly and theatrically tossed everyone out of the room.

He bellowed in his natural heldentenor, "No more visitors for Kerri. All of you. OUT! Do not come back to the hospital unless you are invited by Kerri!"

The man needed a cape to circle at a time like that.

The cantankerous chorus speedily scrambled out of the hospital. Kerri allowed only Lynn and two friends to stay. One of them came to Room 32 and reported to Jeff and me.

"Kerri wants you guys to come in now."

I entered the room to see a delicate and battered young Kerri and a swaddled infant tucked in her embrace. *Mother and Child.* I said, "Kerri, he is perfect. Are you alright?"

She assured me she was fine.

"Can I hold him?" I asked next.

Kerri said, "Of course you can! Here's your son."

I leaned down, carefully took Scotty from Kerri, and kissed her on the cheek.

I felt completely at ease holding the tiny baby boy, tightly wrapped in hospital flannel, seemingly looking up at me, blinking, trying to focus. Little did he know how long I had loved him.

Your soul is a beautiful thing, child.
No emperor received so fair a gift.
The angels wept tonight.

—Gaston Leroux, *Phantom of the Opera*

Loved by Many

Lynn piped "He looks just like Kerri when she was born." Jeff and I held Scotty for the first time with an audience of Kerri, Lynn, Kerri's friends, and nurses. I felt exposed but elated. It was May 13, Jeff's birthday. And now Scotty's birthday.

We texted Bryant a zillion pictures of Scotty. I spoke with him on the phone and bragged, "He is perfectly healthy. Kerri took wonderful care of him."

Kerri said to Bryant, "Jeff and Jody are getting the best baby ever. He is gorgeous."

Bryant asked, "When can I teach him how to be a lady killer?"

I imagine Bryant was grappling with what had just happened, and it had to be tough to live so far away and not be there with Kerri and Scotty. We texted and talked the whole hospital stay.

Jamie let our friends know about Scotty. At 8:40 p.m., she relayed the news.

Hey girls! "It's a boy!" Jody's mom just called me and said everything went well. Jeff had called her and was looking for the diaper bag! I will be anxious to talk to Jody. I will keep you posted.

My friends replied with joy and encouragement. Meredith wrote.

He is safely here! Yay! That is half the battle. Now to start praying for the other half.

Those twelve hours or so we awaited Scotty's birth I focused on Kerri. Once Scotty was born, I focused on my new son and my role as his mother. I entered "survival mode."

Community Baby

Lynn, Kerri, and I took turns holding Scotty. Late that night, I timidly asked the nurses if I could stay in Room 32 overnight. One answered, "Yes, we keep that room blocked for adoption situations."

I wondered why the other staffer told me not to touch anything; maybe she had seen too many adoptions fall through and wanted to wait to see if I even needed the room. This nurse teasingly welcomed me, "Go ahead and contaminate the room. You can stay there unless we run out of labor rooms. Let us know if you need anything."

I gave Scotty his first bottle in Room 32. I felt a surge of parental authority and confidence and told the nurse that I would like for Scotty to stay in the room with me unless Kerri wanted to see him. I explained the close knit relationship Kerri and I held and how we had agreed to share Scotty during the hospital visit.

That first night Kerri endured a great deal of physical pain and exhaustion, so Jeff and I left her alone for the most part. I am sure she was also coming to grips with the magnitude of the birth of her London and the impending adoption of my Scotty. I told her to simply text me if she wanted to see Scotty.

Around 10:00 p.m., Jeff decided to go home. He wanted to share the great news with Houston.

We walked down to Kerri's hospital room to say goodnight. Jeff said, "You did great today, Kerri. I am going home to check on Houston. I'll be back in the morning."

Kerri was holding Scotty. Jeff leaned down, hugged Kerri and kissed Scotty.

As Jeff was about to walk out the door, Kerri called out to him, "Hey Jeff! Happy Birthday."

Jeff turned to face her, smiled ear-to-ear, and said, "No doubt."

May your father and mother be glad;
may she who gave you birth rejoice!

—Proverbs 23:25

Friends are Life Jackets

I walked Jeff to the elevator and went straight back to Kerri's room. She was worn out, so I eagerly took Scotty back down to Room 32 for some private time with me. Finally, after a long, fascinating, exhausting day, I rocked Scotty and looked out the wide hospital window thinking, *This is surreal.* I enjoyed the time with Scotty for a few minutes before Lynn popped her head into the door. She was heading home, too, and wanted a little more time with Scotty. She sat on the rubbery couch in Room 32 and fed Scotty a tiny bottle of Similac.

Lynn cooed, "I'm your Mamaw. I'm your Mamaw. Yes, I am. Yes, I am."

My stomach hurt. I worried that I had promised Lynn too much regarding her future relationship with Scotty. I worried that Lynn would fall in love with Scotty and, over the next few days, convince Kerri to keep him.

When Lynn left around 11:00 p.m., I called one of my best friends for guidance. She adopted her son several years before in a more tumultuous situation. She stood vigil in the hospital nursery guarding her son, who had been born addicted to narcotics.

For days, she prayed the birthmother would stick with the plan and allow her to take the baby home.

She directed me, "Don't you feel one bit bad. Do what you have to do to keep the plan in place for you and Kerri and that baby. This is not about you anymore. It's about Baby Scotty. You are his mama and he needs you. The rest will work itself out."

I trusted her because she understood precisely every aspect of what I was enduring. She had lived it just eight years before. Like any traumatic event, others may understand the hospital adoption experience in an academic, on the page way, but no one can grasp its magnitude like those who have lived it. The inescapable fact that birthparents can change their minds at any point casts a shadow of anxiety over every moment and every encounter.

Jane, the night nurse, talked me into leaving Scotty in the nursery overnight. I was hesitant. She implored, "You are going to need lots of energy tomorrow. It will be a very long day for you. We'll take care of your baby so you can sleep." She was respectful of my position as mother and respectful of the mental labor I had gone through. She understood. I complied.

Physically, I was pain-free, healthy, sporting a hospital bracelet, and perched at an angle in a hospital bed, flipping channels. But I felt like a nut. The room was freezing. I worked up the nerve to ask for another blanket. I felt like a huge imposition. Thankfully, the nurse acted like it was no big deal.

Before I went to bed, I lined up all my shampoo, make-up, and clothes, so that when I awoke, I could spring into action and take care of Kerri and my son.

Friday

For most people,
Friday's just the day before the weekend.
But after this Friday,
the neighborhood'll never be the same.

— "Craig" in *Friday*

Friday morning, I awoke at 5:00 a.m. I *really* needed coffee. I dug into my bag for a granola bar, drank water from the sink, showered, and dressed in record time. I went to the nurses' desk and asked for Scotty. A nurse replied, "He's down the hall with his mom."

Sucker punch.

I guess she did not know what to call Kerri. I understand why most of the hospital staff called her "mom." I suppose saying "birthmother" was awkward for them. Hearing "mom" for Kerri was tough for me. I could not have Scotty at my discretion. I was sharing "my son" with "his mom." I felt alone and did not know what to do. I texted Kerri that I was going to the cafeteria and offered to bring her anything she wanted. She texted back a brief "No thanks."

St. Mary's, like many hospitals, is a hodge-podge of old and new buildings with confusing connections and corridors. Feeling like I was in la-la land, I asked the nurses for directions to the cafeteria. One handed me a map. Using the map and my spatially challenged, worn out brain, I struggled to find the cafeteria. The cyclone whirred in my mind, *Why did she get him so early from the nursery? I need Jeff, but it is too early...I am terrified...I am crazy...She's given no indication of doubt...What should I do?*

I finally found the cafeteria. I sat in the loud room that smelled intermittently of bleach, ammonia, and gravy. I was surrounded by other worried people. I wondered, *Where will all of our hospital stories end? Will we suffer pain? Will we enjoy blissful relief or sorrow?* I ate a biscuit and poured a huge cup of coffee to go. I felt completely, utterly alone. I admitted defeat with the map and hallway maze so I walked outside the hospital to a muggy May morning. I followed the street back to the Women's Pavilion, which held Kerri, Scotty, and our fate.

When I got back to Room 32, I texted Kerri, "Good morning!" She texted back, "Come to my room." I fretfully walked to Kerri's room. She was holding Scotty and taking pictures of him with her phone. I asked her how she was.

Kerri told me she was hurting a lot. She showed me the C-section wound. I thought to myself, *Well, I've ripped this baby right out of her. She's so sweet, and I am selfishly worried about me.*

I kicked back into "service mode" and focused on anyone but me. That settled the cyclone. I spent lots of time alone with Lynn and Scotty, with Kerri's friends and Scotty, but I felt one thousand times better when I was *with* Kerri. Her very presence gave me peace of mind.

Business as Usual, Not

I am not sure when Jeff arrived that morning. My memory is a little fuzzy because I focused so hard on what was happening. I lived in the moment for mental survival.

St. Mary's labor and delivery staff was a well-oiled machine. Nurses performed routine baby tasks amidst our abnormal situation. Scotty's default location was with me in Room 32, so I asked nurses to please send pediatricians and hospital staff to me, not Kerri. Kerri and I agreed that I would make all the decisions, but time and again, staff went to Kerri's room first.

When the audiologist, photographer, St. Mary's baby website coordinator, and pediatricians arrived in Kerri's room, Kerri sent a friend for me. The very first time, I carried Scotty down the hall in my arms.

A nurse stopped me and said, "Ma'am, you can't carry the baby."

In my hypersensitive mode, I reacted, "I'm his adoptive mother."

She forgivingly said, "I know, honey. I just meant that while you are here, you have to roll him in his bed."

She checked my bracelet and sent me back for the cart. Scotty became a one man choo-choo train in his plastic-framed baby bed on wheels, with me as his engineer. I felt conspicuous as I pushed that four-wheeled, boxy chunk of furniture up and down the hallway, past new mothers, staff, and curious strangers.

"Business as usual" again brought out the rawness of adoption. Staff would say to Kerri, "Mom, do you want to hold London while we do this?" or "Congratulations, Mom. London is beautiful," or, to Kerri's mother, "Are you Grandma?"

Kerri always came to my rescue by saying, "Actually, Jody is his mom. She is adopting him from me, and she is naming him Scotty. He is just London for now."

In good humor we coined the phrase "Community Baby." A nurse gave Kerri, Lynn, and me each a string of Scotty's footprints. Kerri and I later laughed about these strange encounters with hospital workers, but at the time, those encounters exhausted me.

When Houston was born, I did not purchase the hospital photo package because, honestly, newborns are usually squish faced and cone headed and the photos are outrageously expensive. But Scotty was a "lady killer," and I could not say no in front of Kerri. So when the photographer came, I bought. I am thankful because the photos are priceless to me now. The photographer had said to Kerri, "Congratulations, Mom. What's his name?" and Kerri had explained, "I call him London but Jody calls him Scotty. She's going to be his mom."

The puzzled photographer looked at me. I explained, "I am adopting him. But Kerri and I are close and pretty laid back. You can ask us anything. We call Scotty our Community Baby!"

As the photographer set up her equipment, Kerri asked if Scotty could wear the gown she brought for him. I agreed. Lynn fished a white infant gown dotted with yellow ducks out of Kerri's bag. I put it on tiny Scotty. He was a calm, obedient, content baby *until* we changed his diaper or clothing. Then he shrieked. Of course, all of us treasured *every* sound and movement our community baby made. We were all instantly in love with him.

The photographer laid Scotty on his stomach and turned his angelic face toward the camera. Before she left, the photographer said to us, like she would to a married couple, "It was really neat to meet you two. You have an incredible story and a beautiful baby."

The day dragged by. Kerri asked, "When is Houston coming?" I had been hesitant to bring Houston in just yet.

I said, "Are you sure?"

She said, "Of course! He needs to meet his baby brother!"

I called my mother and asked her to come to St. Mary's after she picked Houston up from school. I felt overjoyed that my mother would be there soon. I needed her.

Jeff, Mark, Terri, Scotty, and I were in Room 32 when Mama and Houston arrived. Scotty snoozed in his bed-on-wheels while I, starving, gobbled down homemade brownies Terri made us. I hugged Houston, who looked like a teenager compared to Scotty, and took him to Scotty's crib.

"Here he is!"

I picked my swaddled Scotty up and handed him to Mama first. She rocked Scotty for a while. I wanted her to rock *me*—I felt better with her there. Houston marveled at his little brother and fed Scotty a bottle. He asked lots of questions but was equally interested in the waiting room vending machine.

After spending about thirty minutes in Room 32 and feeding five dollars into the vending machine down the hall, Houston excitedly asked, "Can I give Kerri her presents now?" Mama and Houston had stopped at Walgreens drugstore on the way to St. Mary's so Houston could buy Kerri a gift. I texted Kerri to make sure she was ready for the visit. She was. Flanked by my mother and Houston, I rolled Scotty in his bed down the hall.

When we entered Kerri's room, I saw her from my mother's perspective. My mother taught high school English for close to 40 years, so she appreciates the teenage spirit.

Kerri, at twenty-one years old, looked like a petite, pretty high school student who had been through Hell.

My mother hugged Kerri and said, "It's so wonderful to finally meet you. Jody and Jeff just love you." Houston gave Kerri her gifts. He had picked out glittery blue, green, and purple nail polish. Kerri showed my mother her C-section battle wound and the basket of goodies I had brought her. Later, my mother aptly described Kerri as "lovable." In retrospect, I am thankful that Lynn went home before my mother arrived. I think seeing my mother in the grandmother role would have been especially difficult for Lynn. Once more, God took care of the details to spare all of us some discomfort.

After my mother and Houston left, Mark said, "Jeff, you should take Jody out to dinner tonight. You guys need to celebrate!"

I questioned, "What will Kerri think if we leave?"

Mark assured me, "She will see it as a sign of trust. Go somewhere nice."

I felt uneasy leaving the hospital and Scotty, but I did want a break. I told the nurses we were leaving but we would be back. I am sure I sounded crazy. One suggested we go to Bistro by the Tracks, which is two miles from our house. She told us all about it, assuming we had never been and that we did not know our way around town. I guess she figured I was not from Knoxville because I appeared so displaced. I lobbied Jeff to take me home or at least to a restaurant close to home, but he insisted we stay close to the hospital.

We walked out of the Women's Pavilion toward the parking garage and saw Kerri's grandparents headed straight toward us.

I had met them before, briefly, so I said, "Hello! It's nice to see you again." I introduced Jeff. Kerri's grandfather, visibly uncomfortable, looked at us in anguish.

I said, "I promise you we will take wonderful care of him. He is beautiful. Once everything is settled, I will bring him to see you at your house." We hastily exchanged good-byes. He had bought that Winnie-the-Pooh crib bedding for *his* grandson, not *my* son. My thoughts jerked into a rip tide of worry that Kerri's grandfather would influence Kerri to reconsider the adoption. Jeff, unaffected, said, "Jody, calm down. Where do you want to eat?"

We went to Chop House, three miles down Broadway from the hospital. After several minutes alone with Jeff, I felt detached but relaxed. When we got up to leave the restaurant, a man called out, "Hey Hog!" We turned to see one of Jeff's old softball buddies, Ricky, having dinner with his family. He asked, "What are ya'll up to?"

I said, "Well, we have a new baby, born yesterday, that we are adopting. He is at St. Mary's and we are taking a break."

We told him our story. Ricky is Jeff's age and has a teenage daughter. He expressed a little shock, laughed, congratulated us, and rooted us on.

For three days, I relied on texts and quick calls for communication, but I did once hijack the nurses' computer in my room. I was so paranoid I could barely type. Late Friday night I sent the following email:

> *Hello friends and family!*
>
> *In case you haven't heard, Scotty was born Thursday, May 13 (Jeff's birthday)!!! He weighs 7lb and 4 oz and is 19 ¾ inches long. The birthmother had to deliver via C-section so the hospital stay is longer than usual. Not easy for us. I have figured out how to email from the hospital (sneaking) and have very little time alone with the baby so forgive me for not updating you sooner. Thanks again for all your support! Jeff and I feel confident that the birthmother will see the plan through and we'll bring him home soon. We can't wait for you to meet Scotty!*

Happy responses came back, including the following (my two favorites):

You know I am beside myself with excitement for you. I am so happy this has gone so well and you finally have your beautiful baby boy. I can't wait to meet him! I LOVE YOU.
Tobi

THANK GOD!!!!! I AM SO HAPPY FOR YOU ALL!!!! HOPE TO HEAR FROM YOU AGAIN REALLLL SOONNNNNNNNN!!!!! YEAH...XO,
RICHARD AT FEDEX!!!!!

Saturday

*To take something that comes from you, made of you,
and part with it forever and ever.*

—Unknown

I awoke Saturday morning feeling much more confident. My ambitious goal was to take Scotty home that afternoon. If I had "birthed" him we would leave Saturday, so I knew it was *medically* possible. I was forty-eight hours into the hospital and feeling like I belonged there. The nurses warmed up to me, too. Lisa was especially kind. She said I could drink the coffee from the little break room down the hall, thank God.

Thursday, Friday, and Saturday I starved. Waiting parents, if you go to the hospital, pack food and drinks in your bag. Fortunately, I had thrown a few granola bars in my purse. I was one hundred percent engrossed in surviving moment-to-moment and caring for Scotty. Why did I not ask my mother or Jeff to bring me food? I had my car there. I could have hit any drive-through on Broadway.

I did not even have the presence of mind to buy junk food from the vending machines two doors down from my room. I left the hospital four pounds lighter. Kerri and I weighed in at 155 and we left at 135 and 151, respectively!

If I had birthed Scotty, Saturday would have brought lots of visitors. I spent most of Saturday morning alone. Jeff is assistant coach of Houston's Knox Sox baseball team. They were in a tournament so the plan was for Jeff to stay with Houston and his team. Mark, who was coaching his own daughter's softball team that morning, called to let me know he would check on me periodically by phone and come to St. Mary's as soon as the game was over. I drank coffee from the nurse's station, ate my last granola bar, and waited for the pediatrician.

Our doctor arrived around 9:00 a.m. He examined an alert little Scotty and announced, "He is perfect."

I explained to the pediatrician how I really wanted to take Scotty home that day. "Kerri has to stay longer because she had a C-section," I explained to him, "and I don't want Kerri and me to leave at the same time—I think that would be awkward and difficult for Kerri. What do you think?"

"Well, Scotty is perfectly fine to go home today," the pediatrician said. "I see no reason for him to stay one more minute."

Thrilled, I asked for a favor. I wanted Scotty home but I wanted to respect his birthmother. "Can we go down to Kerri's room, with Scotty? Will you explain things to her so that she is part of the decision? If she says she wants him to stay, he'll stay." The doctor agreed.

Again, Scotty cruised the hallway with me at the wheel. The pediatrician treated Kerri with reverence and compassion. He simply said, "This boy is healthy and ready to go home. I would like for him to leave today, but Jody said that it is up to you. What do you think, Kerri?"

Kerri said, "Well, if it's what's better for him, then it's fine with me." I offered to bring Scotty back to the hospital if Kerri felt like she needed to see him the next day. I meant it.

"I'll do the release paperwork, and you can leave in a couple of hours," our considerate pediatrician told us.

I figured we would be home by 11:30 a.m. Kerri asked me to leave Scotty with her for a while. Elated, I went to Room 32 to pack and call Jeff. He did not answer. I called one of the Knox Sox mothers and left a message. I kept calling until I talked to Dana.

"The doctor said Scotty can come home as soon as Jeff gets here to sign hospital forms and the Bethany placement papers. Where is Jeff?"

"He's out on the field. Oh, my gosh! I will tell him! We will make him leave right now!"

I imagined the Knox Sox moms rushing the fence. I tease Dana that, in full competition mode, she can climb the backstop to scream at the umpires without dropping her hot dog.

Dana said she yelled, "JEFF, YOU HAVE TO LEAVE! JODY SAID IT'S TIME TO BRING SCOTTY HOME! HURRY JEFF!" That would have been a great time for fans to do the wave.

When I recently asked my friend Kelly what happened at the baseball field she said, "I remember all the moms going in to panic mode and all the dads saying 'Ok, well the game is almost over.' That's the difference between moms and dads!"

Dana promised to bring Houston home later and confirmed Jeff was headed to the hospital. I called Mark, and he too was on his way.

Alone again, I sat in my room, rocked in the rocking chair, and waited. I heard a knock at the door. Expecting Mark or Terri, I said, "Come in." I was surprised to see Kerri, settled in her wheelchair, cradling Scotty. Kerri's friend pushed her near me and left.

Kerri and I sat, she in her wheelchair, I in the hospital's hardwood rocker, between the single bed and the window. I had opened the blinds earlier so sunlight could warm Room 32.

The metal-molded window framed a mundane view. Three floors below the window, a long sloped sidewalk sat parallel to a two way street. Across the street, trucks and cars dotted a charcoal parking lot. A graveled afterthought of a parking area lay above the more formal spaces. I saw no people. The only life and movement came from a row of trees planted equidistantly along the sidewalk. The scene looked uninteresting and ordinary. But the events inside the building supported by the parking spots, street, and sidewalk were extraordinary.

Kerri and I faced one another in front of that bright hospital window on that beautiful May morning and talked for a long time. Isolated and insulated by the hospital, I felt secure as I observed my son and his birthmother together. I also felt compelled to witness to Kerri, remembering that Mark said I was the closest thing to Jesus that Kerri knew. I could have seized that moment to share scripture with the frail girl in front of me, but I thought, *Who am I to tell this angel about sacrifice? She loves Scotty, unconditionally, infinitely, by nature's default. She has given up a life with him, for him. She is the closest thing to Jesus I have ever known.*

I cannot remember what we said to one another but I do remember that, as I watched Kerri hold, talk to, and kiss Scotty, I thought of the hymn lyrics, "There's a sweet, sweet spirit in this place." Those moments with Kerri were a sacred privilege.

What NOW?

Possession is nine tenths of the law.

—Unknown

Kerri, Scotty, and I were still together in my room when Mark arrived at St. Mary's. We had to complete the following tasks before we could take Scotty home: a nurse needed to review discharge instructions, Jeff and I had to discuss and sign the final child placement documents with Mark (including pay the placement fee), and Kerri had to say goodbye.

When Terri arrived, she delicately suggested that Kerri take Scotty to her room and spend some "last hospital time" alone with him while Jeff and I completed the paperwork. Kerri heeded the advice. Kerri has never told me about her last minutes alone with Scotty. I have never asked her to, because I figure those moments were supremely painful and should remain private. In that hour that day, Scotty was *London*. He was Kerri's son, legally and emotionally, and in her physical possession.

She had carried and cared for him for thirty-nine weeks. I imagine those minutes, though cherished, were agonizing. I imagine no hour in the rest of Kerri's life will be as intense.

Terri went to counsel Kerri.

Jeff, Mark, and I sat down to go over the paperwork and could have completed it in twenty minutes, but, because Kerri and Terri were talking privately, Kerri's mother and friends kept popping into Room 32. I was annoyed at the intermittent visits because I *really* wanted to move things along. Mark, on the other hand, demonstrated nothing but calm consideration for Kerri's friends and family members. He asked them questions and showed genuine interest in their personal stories. I was on a mission, but I was in awe of his compassion. He noticed that they, too, were seeking to understand the magnitude of this experience, and he ministered to them while Jeff and I sat, held papers, and waited. Mark Akers deserves a halo.

We finally finished the paperwork.

Terri came back from Kerri's room to update us. "Scotty is in the nursery. Kerri said good-bye to him and wants to see you guys before you leave."

All boxes checked, we were ready to go, right?

I went to the nurses' station and announced, "We are all finished. Kerri has said goodbye to Scotty and is grieving so please don't take him back down there."

A nurse said she would get the paperwork together on their end. Mark went down to Kerri's room.

Terri, Jeff, and I sat in Room 32 and waited for a signal to leave.

A nurse, whom I had never met, entered the room and spoke sharply.

"We need to do a few more things before the baby can go home. A pediatrician needs to examine him."

"What do you mean? Our family pediatrician was here at 9:00 a.m. and completed paperwork to release him."

"Well, he is *your* pediatrician. One of *our* pediatricians has to sign off."

"What? Why? I've never heard of that."

At that moment, I sat on the edge of the bed, dropped my face into my hands, and wept for the first time in the hospital. The nurse was so cold. All of the other nurses had been nice. Why did she do that? Did she have some personal issue with adoption? I wondered, *Why is she placing this last, needless hurdle in our way? Why is she dragging this out?*

"I sent the baby back to the mother's room until the doctor arrives to do the examination," the nurse said.

I broke down. "He is *not* supposed to go back down there. Kerri has already said goodbye to the baby. You are torturing that sweet soul down the hall."

Terri remained calm. Jeff looked at me like I was falling apart. We were powerless. We did *more* waiting. When the cold nurse sent Scotty back to Kerri's room, Kerri apparently lost it and refused, "No, I've already said goodbye! Please leave me alone."

Mark calmed me down. Terri suggested Jeff spend this odd remaining time alone with Kerri, and he did. Jeff stayed alone with her for a long time. Kerri later told me that Jeff truly kept her from crumbling.

At least another hour passed as the St. Mary's pediatrician examined Scotty. Terri went to the nurses' station for a few minutes, came back and said, "Okay—we are ready to GO!"

A nurse brought Scotty in from the nursery. I had brought a special gown for him to go home in, but Terri wanted to act fast. "Let's just get him in this car seat and get you home!" It was a good call. Mark babysat Scotty so I could say goodbye to Kerri. With Terri, I walked one last time to Kerri's hospital room, where Jeff and Kerri still talked.

I hugged Kerri, kissed her cheek, and with a trembling voice said, "You have no idea what you have done for us. Thank you. Thank you. Thank you."

She, in her tiny voice, responded, "You're welcome. I love you guys. I couldn't ask for better parents for my son."

We both embraced her. I said, "We love you, too" and we left.

Terri stayed behind.

Jeff and I returned to our room and said good-bye to Mark. Jeff picked up Scotty, securely harnessed into his polka-dot carrier, and we left Room 32 and walked toward the elevator.

A nurse spotted us and said, "Wait."

I thought but did not say, *Are you freaking kidding me?*

She continued, "Someone has to escort you. Cameron will walk you down."

It was 3:00 p.m., and I was absolutely dog-tired. In my weariness, I did not realize Cameron was a fellow church member, or that Houston was in choir with her child. I knew her, but I did not recognize her in that moment. I was a basket case.

Once we were finally out the door, Jeff and I walked up the sidewalk to the parking garage.

I said, "Can you believe this really happened? Can you believe that we actually have this baby boy?"

Jeff answered, "I know."

"It's unbelievable. How do you feel?"

"I may never meet my own birthmother, but at least I got to meet Scotty's."

My six-foot-two masculine husband cried all the way to the car.

Jeff snapped Scotty's "bucket" into place in Big Red's backseat and said, "See you at home."

I should have followed him. I should have had a driver! Disoriented and crying, I looped and looped and looped through the parking garage until I finally found the exit.

Driving away from the hospital, I felt free. I was anxious to get home with Scotty, looking forward to holding him in my rocking chair, in my living room, with Houston, Jeff, and my mother nearby.

I was happy, but all I could think of was Scotty's brave birthmother, still at St. Mary's, in her labor and delivery unit hospital room, without her baby.

Courage is not simply one of the virtues,
but the form of every virtue at the testing point.

—C.S. Lewis

High Tide

I knew that once we got home, friends would show up to meet Scotty, so I called my mother who was already at my house. I asked her to get Scotty's bath ready so we could scrub the hospital off him and dress him in a soft gown before anyone arrived.

As soon as I brought Scotty into the house, I stripped off his clothes and took him to my bathroom where Mama waited with Johnson & Johnson's Bedtime Bath and a pallet of soft white towels. I had just laid him on the towels and started the water when neighbor Allyn rang the doorbell. I heard her say to Jeff, "I saw you come up the driveway, and I couldn't resist! Where is Scotty?"

My mother and Allyn could not get close enough to the soaped-up infant squirming on the counter. I boxed them out and bathed him. Allyn went to pick up some wine.

I took Scotty into his room to dress him.

Mama sat on the big bed while I put Scotty in a soft, clean gown and tiny booties to match. She asked me, "Jody, how do you feel?"

I held Scotty up, and, like a mama cat, licked him across the top of the head. She died laughing. We were so happy.

Come One, Come All!

I rushed to put Kerri's Winnie-the-Pooh sheets on Scotty's baby bed. They did not match his arts and crafts nursery, but I promised Kerri photos of his first days at home and wanted her and her grandfather to know I appreciated the bedding.

Allyn brought back two boxes of wine and the celebration began. When her husband John and his daughter Ashley held Scotty, they kept repeating, "He's so tiny." We introduced Scotty to several more friends that day. Saturday started out rough but became a long-awaited, joyful afternoon.

Jeff lit Facebook on fire. Of course, folks wanted pictures, but we were advised not to share any photos just yet out of respect for the birth family. Our family was at the happy end of the adoption spectrum; Kerri's family was at the other end. Plus, Scotty was legally Kerri's child under the guardianship of Bethany Christian Services, and under our custodial care. We were not the primary decision makers yet.

Thrilled and relieved, we soberly understood this was a "legal risk placement." Our friends and family, however, simply celebrated and took turns holding a sweet baby boy.

In 1963, Jeff's parents brought him home from a foster mother. He was ten weeks old. Mrs. Dyer told me that Jeff's crib was in the corner of his nursery; she slept on a twin bed on one wall and Mr. Dyer slept in a twin bed on the other.

The three narrow beds connected like circled wagons to protect the innocent. When describing her weight loss of several pounds the first few weeks Jeff was home, she said, "All I could do was take care of Jeff, and I stayed up all night waiting for Jeff to wake up!"

Late Saturday night, I swaddled Scotty in a soft thin blanket and laid him in that crib on which I had prayed four months earlier.

Like my in-laws decades before, I slept in a bed beside the crib. Between us, a rooster lamp, a gift from Jamie, perched on a blue table. I laid Scotty width-wise in his bed so we could face each other. The rooster and I kept a watchful eye on Scotty all night. Scotty was calm and beautiful with an olive complexion and slate gray eyes. He stared right back at me.

The Placement Ceremony

The LORD has done great things for us,
and we are filled with joy.

—Psalm 126:3

As is customary, Bethany hosted a Placement Ceremony for our family and friends to meet Scotty. On Monday, May 17th, a few dozen folks gathered in the same room where Jeff and I had attended Waiting Families support group meetings. I hid upstairs with Scotty as Jeff, Houston, Mark, and Terri greeted friends and family. Houston kept coming upstairs and opening the door. He was walking on air and quite impatient. The last time he came, he brought my cousin Toby's then three-year-old daughter Rosalind. I said, "Come on in and see your baby cousin!" I lifted the blanket covering Scotty's carrier, there in case someone spotted us early. Rosalind peeked in at the sleeping four-day-old infant and asked, "Is that your baby, Jody?"

"YES!"

Mark began the ceremony by explaining the domestic adoption process to the crowd. He wanted them to understand the rigorous path to adoption and to appreciate what we had been through all those years. Then Jeff, Houston, Scotty, and I walked into the room as a family of four. I held Scotty in a white, hand-stitched blanket. He wore a soft blue gown embroidered with a tiny white lamb and the words "His little lamb." On the back, just below the neck, was Psalm 23: *The LORD is my shepherd.* For several minutes, I walked around the room, showing Scotty off to a packed house of family and friends.

Dr. Barron, our family friend and former pastor, led us in prayer. Mark and Terri told our story to those who had supported us and prayed for us for so long. He explained why Kerri chose us, how we had ministered to her, how our relationship developed, and what an open adoption looks like. Mark described Jeff in the hospital as "The Man" and explained how much Jeff helped Kerri. Terri chimed in with anecdotal commentary about how well Kerri and I got along and how our relationship comforted each of us. They consistently reminded the audience that Kerri and Bryant love Scotty and have a tough time in front of them. I recall looking around that room, first seeing a sobbing Kiki, who had helped me begin the research that would put us on the adoption path. Jeff's parents, my mother, aunts, uncles, cousins, friends, pastors, and Houston's friends looked purely delighted.

The scene that impressed me most, however, was an entire wall of men. Houston's coaches and Jeff's buddies stood from corner to corner like a protective shield of Christian role models.

After his presentation, Mark asked, "Jody, do you have anything you would like to add?"

I answered, "Of course!" and everyone chuckled. I said something along the lines of, "The adoption process took two full years, but we began trying for Scotty when Houston was nine months old. When people ask me how long it took for us to get Scotty, my answer will be *eight years*. This has been an eight-year journey for us, and I want you all to know that I appreciate every word of encouragement, every prayer. When we were in that hospital, I was under so much stress, but time after time, one of you would call and say or text exactly what I needed to hear. Please keep Kerri in your prayers. She is a sweet person who has done something momentous. She is grieving. Throughout the adoption wait, thanks to Mark, Terri, and Lauren at Bethany, Jeff and I became mentally prepared. But we are spiritually overwhelmed."

Mark then asked Jeff if he wanted to say anything.

Jeff, true to form, replied, "I'm good."

Everyone laughed. To close out the ceremony, family and friends circled around Scotty, Houston, Jeff, and me. Mark prayed a beautiful message of thanks. As he prayed, Scotty sighed in peaceful slumber in my arms.

Afterward, friends and family took pictures and took turns holding Scotty. My Aunt Judy, who was "busting at the seams" to get hold of Scotty, proclaimed, "So much for genetics! That's the prettiest baby ever born in this family!"

The scene was happy and chaotic and, again, my presence of mind was lackluster. I neglected to have anyone take a family photo at such a special occasion. Waiting mother, assign someone the job of photographer.

We left the Bethany office and everyone came to our house to celebrate. Houston told my mother, "This is the greatest day of my life."

And, has thou slain the Jabberwock?
Come to my arms, my beamish boy!
O frabjous day! Callooh! Callay!'
He chortled in his joy.

`Twas brillig, and the slithy toves
Did gyre and gimble in the wabe;
All mimsy were the borogoves,
And the mome raths outgrabe.

—Lewis Carroll, *Alice's Adventures in Wonderland*

Home But Not Home Free

Our visitors felt nothing but exuberance over this long-awaited baby's arrival. But Jeff and I had just endured something traumatic and could not quite celebrate with the same uninhibited enthusiasm. We enjoyed introducing Scotty as our son, but Kerri's rights were not yet terminated and would not be for days. We were home, but not home free.

As family and friends came and went, Kerri, Bryant, Jeff and I texted back and forth for several days. Kerri was still recovering in the hospital. Her Bethany counselor Lauren was back and helping her cope.

When friends or family noticed me texting Kerri, they panicked and threw out lots of questions. They would ask "What is she saying to you?" or "Does talking to her make you nervous?" or "When do you have to see her again?" Worse were "Why are you still talking to her?" and "Do you *have* to talk to her?"

The most common question was "Can she take him back?" to which I begrudgingly replied, "Yes, until her rights are terminated," knowing I would then have to explain the legal process for parental rights termination in Tennessee.

I sensed that many of my family members found my easiness in talking to and about Kerri unsettling.

Friends remarked that they did not think, if in a similar situation, they could remain so communicative, so open, so vulnerable. I often found myself convincing and consoling others.

I hope readers understand that I know that my attitude during the wait, in the hospital, and at home those first few days may seem pessimistic. I trusted Kerri throughout the process. She never showed a sign of doubt. However, I gave birth to Houston and I intimately understood what it would be like for her to see her London at his first breath. I also knew Kerri was confronting an ever-present undertow: her family's influence and grief. All along, I knew that if Kerri changed her mind, I, as a mother, though heartbroken, would understand why.

How Do You Say Thank-You?

As the women in my life came to see Scotty, I asked them to write a note to Kerri in a purple-flowered journal. In my Dear Birthmother Letter, I promised Kerri that Scotty would have a wonderful life. I wanted her to see that she is honored and respected by many people, not just Jeff and me. I also wanted to build empathy. By communicating directly with Kerri on paper, my friends personally experienced relating to Scotty's birthmother, and they gained a better sense of Kerri's and my relationship. The exercise quelled many of their questions and much of their confusion. I enjoyed watching my friends grapple with the little project and found their consistent expression of admiration toward Kerri uplifting. My friend Amber confirmed, "This is hard! Jody, I am getting a glimpse at what you've been through. I don't know how we made it!"

From my mother, "Grandmama",

Dear Kerri,
I am watching two speedy little squirrels run up and down the branches of the huge maple tree in front of my old farmhouse as I write to you. Over 100 years ago, when the original two rooms of this house were built, the tree was planted far too close and directly in front

of the front door, so I sometimes feel like I live in a big tree house. It is totally quiet and safe here, so Scotty will be able to run freely, laugh loudly, and explore endlessly the vast woods, the gentle creek, and the ancient barn. I promise to always keep him out of harm's way.

When I think about you and your determination to do your very best for your beloved son, I find it difficult to adequately express my respect and admiration. You are STRONG. You are UNSELFISH. You are SOULFUL. You are REAL. Getting to know you through Jody and Jeff has made me privy to this. You live life, and you understand other people and their circumstances because, as Jody has told me, "Kerri gets it."

My precious Kerri, thank you. I wish you "a rainbow, a star, and red roses wherever you are" (Theme from Butch Cassidy and the Sundance Kid*).*
Love Always,
Donna

From Jeff's mother, called "Bop" by Houston and my nieces Ellie and Anna Kate,

Dear Kerri,

Late this afternoon, as I left the home of Jody, Jeff, Houston, and Scotty, a rain had just fallen and the sun was coming out. I looked for a rainbow but there was not one for me at that moment. As I drove I thought, There is *a rainbow in our lives that started on May 13, 1963 and came into full color on May 13, 2010.*

I thought of two beautiful, loving and caring young women who came into the hearts of our family on those dates. Brave young women who made very

~ 197 ~

painful decisions in their lives, and by doing so, we received blessings beyond description.

I believe God has a plan for each of us. When I held Scotty yesterday, he was so beautiful, so perfect, so precious. My heart races with the memory of the first time I held Jeff in my arms. The unbelievable love that came instantly with Jeff and that came instantly with Scotty. God's plans and God's love. My only regret is that Jeff's birthmother does not know our family. She does not know the wonderful young man he is today— the son, the brother, the cousin, the son-in-law, the friend, the husband, and now the father of two precious boys. I am very grateful you can know all of these things about Scotty if you so choose.

Love,

Bop

Court

Remember that adoption is an industry. Well, not only does the process involve doctors, insurance companies, social workers, employers, the police, veterinarians, and drug labs, it also involves the court system. When you "birth" a baby, the hospital initiates the birth certificate and social security number forms, and you may add the baby to your insurance with a simple phone call. The first step toward Scotty's becoming legally ours was for Kerri to terminate her rights in court. In the state of Tennessee, the birthfather may surrender his rights at any time during or after the pregnancy. Bryant, thoughtfully, did so in February, months before Scotty was born. The birthmother, however, may only file the intent to waive parental rights once the baby is four days old.

Kerri had to recover from a C-section but felt well enough to go to court on Friday, May 21. Once Kerri filed the intent, ten business days had to pass and her rights would terminate. The tenth business day could not fall on a weekend or holiday. So, June 1 was The Day. Lauren called me and said that Kerri really wanted me to come with her to court. I was shocked because I imagined that would be a harrowing day for Kerri. She said she wanted my support and to see the baby, so we had our first post-placement meeting at Starbucks, and then I followed Lauren and Kerri to the courthouse.

I sat on a bench in the hallway and held Scotty while Kerri and Lauren met with the family court judge. A haggard-looking old man struck up a conversation with me. He told me how he could not take care of his kids so the court took them away. He asked what I was doing there, and I hesitantly told him.

He remarked, "It's good she has you."

I spoke to the man while Kerri was in the judge's chambers, and I appreciated the ironic diversion. Kerri and Lauren came into the hallway and Kerri appeared to be just fine. I do not know how she was so strong. She took lots of pictures of Scotty, and we parted ways. I figured I would not see her for several weeks.

Again, I was wrong.

Safe in the Outfield

Gird up now thy loins like a man;
for I will demand of thee, and answer thou me.

—Job 38:3

The *next* day, Saturday, May 22, Houston and the Knox Sox had ballgames. I planned to stay home with nine-day-old Scotty and relax. Around 9:00 a.m., Kerri texted me, "Hey, is there any way you can bring the baby out to see me? I am having a hard time and I really need to see him."

The first thing that came to mind was what that lady said at dinner just a few weeks before about how a friend's baby was picked up by the social worker at their house because the birthmother changed her mind.

Mama, Jeff, and Houston were at the ball field. I was completely alone and completely freaking out. I replied, "Of course. I will leave here right now." I wanted to get there and get it over with so I would not have to worry any longer than necessary.

I threw Pampers, wipes, and formula into Scotty's diaper bag, buckled him into the car seat, and sobbed down I-640 and across Western Avenue into Kerri's neighborhood.

Just before I got to her house, I stopped to fix my makeup and to pray for peace of mind. I thought of Job 38:3: *Gird up now thy loins like a man; for I will demand of thee, and answer thou me.*

Minutes later, I knocked on the door only to feel a sweet Kerri embrace me, then Scotty. She said, "I just needed to see him. I missed you guys."

We stayed an hour or so. When I left, I felt selfish and relieved. I felt wrung out like a kitchen towel used to soak up one of Houston's giant Kool-Aid spills.

Instead of going home, I drove to the baseball field. Mama met me in the parking lot. The game had already started and Houston was at bat just as Mama and I rolled Scotty in his polka-dot stroller to the outfield shade. Then, from the stands, "there rose a lusty yell." We heard "WAY TO GO HOUSTON!" and saw a ball fly over the fence. Houston had hit his first homerun at Scotty's first baseball game!

Later that week, I emailed one of the Team Adoption mothers, Talania, who adopted two of her children, asking her to pray for Kerri as she was in lots of physical and emotional pain and for me as I waited for Kerri's parental rights to end. She wrote back.

> *Yes, I feel your pain and joy. It's hard getting to know a birth mom and wanting her to be happy but knowing that isn't possible right now. It's bittersweet for sure. Both our boys' birth moms are doing well and do not regret the decisions they made. It was just hard letting go and transitioning.*

Encouragement from mothers who have "been there" is priceless. Waiting parents, take note of all of the tiny, huge, beautiful, painful, and miraculous moments in your journey.

Early one morning a few days after that visit with Kerri, I was making coffee, and I looked out my kitchen window to see a mother deer and her two babies in my backyard. The doe and I looked right at each other. We were both protective, both afraid. She would lead her two babies safely across the road. I would love and care for Scotty, knowing Kerri's rights would not terminate until June 1 at 5:00 p.m., when Scotty was nineteen days old.

Unfathomable Love and Consideration

The storm starts, when the drops start dropping
When the drops stop dropping
then the storm starts stopping.

—Dr. Seuss, *Oh, The Places You'll Go!*

On June 1, 2010, at 4:15 p.m., I sat in the same chair where I had rocked Houston eight years earlier. I held a sleeping Scotty.

Kerri texted me, "I just wanted you to know that he is yours. I know my time is almost up and didn't want you to worry another minute. I could not have picked better parents for my child. I know I did the right thing."

I sat, stunned by how, while drowning in her own grief, she threw me a rope of thoughtfulness and compassion.

Back To Normal, But With My Baby

Friends and family rejoiced in relief that Scotty was finally one hundred percent, not fifty-fifty, ours! My church friends and "sports mamas" threw Scotty beautiful showers.

We spent summer days on the farm and at baseball fields. All we had to do to formally adopt Scotty was wait six months, host three home visits with Mark, and then file the final adoption decree to get Scotty's new birth certificate with Jeff and Jody Dyer listed as his parents. We were finally home free; we just had to complete a little more paperwork.

During a visit with Kerri and Lynn that summer, Lynn insisted I take the Pack-N-Play from her bedroom to have at my house. I already had Houston's old playpen, but, astounded and relieved by Lynn's immense, emotional, *personal* offer, I accepted the Pack-N-Play with joyful gratitude.

She was letting go.

Bryant Meets Our Son

In July we flew Bryant down to meet Scotty and us. This was Jeff's idea. A few weeks after we brought Scotty home, Jeff, who had also learned to text, sent Bryant a message that we would love to meet him and that we would buy him a round trip ticket to Tennessee.

Bryant had a new job so he could only come for a three-day visit. Kerri was ecstatic. She and Bryant still held deep affection for one another, though strained by the separation and, obviously, the trauma involved in the pregnancy and adoption. They had not seen each other in months. As usual, Jeff was relaxed and I was nervous.

Bryant spent most of his visit with Kerri. Jeff, Houston, Scotty, and I met them at Bryant's hotel where we talked a while. Then we all went to lunch. We passed rolls and Scotty around the table. Mostly, we talked about Bryant's interests, which included movies, music, and baseball, and tried to get to know him. He lives so far away; I knew this may be the only time, for a long time, that I would be with him. So I took mental notes to share with Scotty.

Later, Scotty and I escorted Kerri and Bryant to the airport to say good-bye. Though Bryant, like Jeff, appeared unruffled throughout the visit, I wondered what this was like for him. Scotty has Bryant's elfish ears, olive complexion, and dark eyes. What must it have been like for him to meet his child and his child's parents and then leave? I think the visit was good for all of us. We continue to have a friendly relationship of mutual trust and respect with Bryant.

Legal and Real

For the next few months the only burdens I faced were small happy tasks of protecting Scotty's privacy. At the pediatrician's office, the nurse called out "London, Room..." All of his shot records, daycare notes, and prescriptions read "London," not Scotty. He would not have a Social Security number until the adoption was finalized. I no longer had the underlying fear of losing Scotty to his birthparents, but I still had to explain things. I went round and round with the insurance company.

We went on a family beach trip in August when Scotty was three months old. I found it ironic that airport officials made me remove my shoes and empty my handbag into a basket, but they never questioned my parental authority over the snoozing infant I carried in a cloth sling. I was ready to defensively whip out the "Statement of Adoption" from Bethany Christian Services that documented my custodial rights to Scotty, but Scotty and I cruised through three airports without a hitch. I carried the "Statement of Adoption" from Bethany Christian Services in my wallet for over a year.

Our good friends Warren and Jennifer gave us sweet, generous gifts. An attorney, Warren performed all of the legal work to finalize Scotty's adoption without charge. Jennifer took on the job of official adoption day photographer.

On April 6, 2011, we went to Knox Chancery Court. I drove Mama, Scotty, and me to the courthouse, parked at a meter, and neurotically overpaid by a dollar. I called Jeff several times to make sure he and Houston were on their way. We all met Mark, Warren, and Jennifer inside the courthouse and proceeded to the judge's office. Jeff asked me, "Why are you acting so uptight?"

"I feel engaged and almost married," I joked. That may sound ridiculous at that point, but many of my adoptive-mom friends said they felt the same way.

Mama brought chocolate-filled Easter baskets for Warren, Mark, and Houston.

The judge appointed us Scotty's legal parents, just as though I had given birth to him.

Jennifer took pictures of all of us inside the judge's office and outside on the pretty spring day. As I type this, I am looking at the photo collage Jennifer thoughtfully made for me. She included pictures of Jeff and me, right hands in the air, swearing to be good parents, a sweet picture of Houston holding his baby brother in front of yellow tulips, and a photo of the judge signing the adoption decree. Warren treated all of us to breakfast.

That was one of the happiest mornings of my life.

I told my mother, "Now I understand how Gapetto felt. Scotty is a real boy!"

An Open Adoption in Uncharted Waters

And as for you, brothers,
never tire of doing what is right.

—Thessalonians 3:13

I can share numerous details of my story with you since I have an "open domestic adoption" with my child's birthmother. I define open adoption as a relationship of mutual respect and communication when the adopted child and his or her birth family know each other. I am not legally bound to communicate or continue a relationship with Kerri or her family: my obligation is simply one of promise and moral commitment.

I am an approachable, candid, talkative woman, so an open adoption matches my personality. My beliefs have taught me to be tolerant and forgiving. It is understandable, due to misinformation, that many waiting parents and their families fear open adoption. Most questions I answer these days relate to Kerri's and my current relationship. People typically find perplexing the logistics and strain of continued communication with the birth parents after adoption.

Kerri and I are not some Cornball Express buddy-buddy situation. There have been times where I have had to set boundaries. For example, Kerri is single, and I am wary of introducing Scotty to any of her male friends. I also limit Scotty's visits with Kerri's extended family. Kerri and I discuss appropriate precedents and expectations for the future. We have made mistakes, but Kerri, Bryant, Jeff, and I have always shown each other respect and understanding. Fortunately, Bethany counselors are available and happy to help us. We navigate the open adoption course like explorers, since none of us know people with adoptions as open as Scotty's.

I am proud to call Kerri my friend and I believe it is a privilege to share this expedition with such a resilient young woman.

Baby's First Year

The loss-laden wounds of infertility and adoption trauma never quite heal. A dear friend, whose two adopted children are exceptional and thriving, confessed to me that she still grieves that she never experienced pregnancy and childbirth. I still scan my gynecologist's waiting room for pregnant bellies attached to bandless hands. I still feel cheated and annoyed when I meet pregnant teenagers.

In August, I began my required semester-long student teaching assignment. Scotty was only three-months old; he and I flew home from the beach trip the night before I had to begin work. My mother came to Knoxville each day to care for Scotty and be home when Houston hopped off the school bus. Jeff and I could not yet afford daycare, financially or emotionally. (As a matter of fact, we are still paying off some of our adoption expenses.) Scotty was waking at midnight and 4:00 a.m. I hauled my sleep-deprived body, aching with newly employed yet aging muscles, through scalding showers and heavy doses of concealer and coffee to a local high school for eighteen weeks.

On my first day, in my first class, I met Angela (I have changed her name in this book to protect her privacy). She was seventeen, living in foster-care, and eight months pregnant. I thought, *I could not be in the same room with this girl every day if I did not already have Scotty.*

Angela was one of several pregnant girls I met there. In another class, a sixteen-year-old student was the mother of a ten-month old boy.

Ashamed of my unsuccessful attempts to get Scotty to sleep through the night, I desperately asked the teenager for advice. My colleagues found the scene amusing.

I remarked to another student once, "Wow, there sure are a lot of pregnant girls at this school."

She confirmed, "Yep. We are #1 in the county for babies and car wrecks!"

I talked to Angela whenever I could about her plans. She would keep the baby. I brought Lynn's Pack-N-Play to school and gave it to Angela. We met in the parking lot after school. I pulled the bulky apparatus from the back of Big Red and watched Angela and her foster sister lift it onto the school bus to take home.

Ironically (or not, considering the student body was "#1 in babies") the next fall I bumped into yet another student from that same class. She was pushing a double stroller with two tiny baby boys inside.

All the times I saw or talked to one of the pregnant teens, I thought of the women in waiting at Bethany, and I felt resentment and frustration on their behalf. I still do.

The first year after Scotty was born, Kerri and I followed a mutually agreeable plan coordinated by Bethany social workers. Each of us completed a form outlining our expectations regarding updates on Scotty's growth and development, photos of Scotty, and visits. At the beginning of each of Scotty's first twelve months, I completed a short update form called the Adoptive Family Monthly Report detailing all things Scotty. On the form, I wrote about Scotty's travels to Houston's Knox Sox baseball and Kings basketball games, our trip to the beach with Jeff's side of the family, how Houston helped take care of Scotty, and how much family and friends enjoyed meeting and spending time with Scotty.

I documented his sleeping and eating habits. I recorded his physical, emotional, social, and behavioral development. I remember that on the first form I wrote about how my Uncle Steve deemed Scotty "Smiling Boy" because he smiled constantly from the time he was one week old! I also enclosed at least eight pictures for Bryant and eight pictures for Kerri. I tried to include photos of Scotty interacting with Houston, cousins, friends, and Jeff and me. I expect it was hard but beneficial for Kerri and Bryant to see Scotty in Jeff's and my embraces. I dropped the packages off at Bethany each month, and Mark forwarded them on to Kerri and Bryant.

My direct communication with Kerri continued via text messages for the first several months. I updated Kerri and Bryant after each of Scotty's check-ups. I sent picture messages of Scotty that might amuse them. I thought of Kerri, and still do, throughout the day.

If Kerri wanted, or sometimes needed, to see Scotty, she simply called me, and we arranged a time to meet. The visits mostly served to help Kerri heal and put her mind at ease. Often, it was most convenient for me to just go to her mother Lynn's home. Once, when I took Scotty to Lynn's, several of Kerri's extended family members showed up, unannounced to me. That made me a little apprehensive, and I honestly expressed my concern to Kerri.

Just after Christmas, Jeff, Houston, Scotty, and I went to see Kerri, Lynn, and Lynn's parents. We exchanged gifts. I was nervous. I am not sure why. I had met all of Kerri's small family several times, they had no legal rights, and they were always sweet and obliging toward me. I think the whole situation, if I meditated on the magnitude of what Kerri and Bryant did for us, still overwhelmed me emotionally. But the evening turned out lovely. Kerri gave me a bracelet decorated with baby bottle, pram, and teddy bear charms. Lynn gave me a necklace holding a clear heart-shaped locket containing my family's birthstones.

I gave them copies of the beautiful newborn picture of Scotty in his yellow duck gown, taken on Kerri's hospital bed. After that meeting I feared I had set an unrealistic precedent. My fears multiplied when Kerri's family pressured her to have a first birthday party for Scotty in May. To ease some pressure off Kerri, I agreed. Jeff had to work so my mother came with me for moral support. We met at a restaurant and shared a meal, a birthday cake, and our sweet Scotty. I sensed tension between Kerri and her family as they were reminded of their loss of this child. I recalled how my friend coached me not to underestimate the loss suffered by Kerri's extended family. My mother respectfully toned down her goo-goos and gah-gahs toward Scotty while we were there, but I wondered what Lynn felt as she watched my mother be "Grandmama" to Scotty. I know it had to be hard for her, but I think it was good, too. My mother and Kerri's family got along well.

Scotty's "official" first birthday party took place in Nashville with Jeff's family. We celebrated with the traditional Dyer first birthday cake, baked in the shape of a little lamb by Jeff's mother. Scotty, like many one-year-olds, was disinterested in the cake and uncomfortable in the pale blue smocked jumper he wore. But he was a hit at the party with his constant smile and happy demeanor. Mr. Dyer, Jeff's brother Jay, Jeff, and our niece Anna Kate were all born in May. We had one big party, but Scotty was the real star of that show!

Baby's Second Year

As I type this section, Scotty is two years and one month old. Houston is reading Sam's Speedy Fire Truck to him in the living room. I just heard Scotty chime in with "doggy" and "water."

A couple of weeks ago, Scotty and I visited Kerri and her family at Kerri's grandparents' home to celebrate Scotty's second birthday. Scotty did not want to get out of the car when we first arrived. He clung to me. I felt sorry for Kerri, but I know she understood. He probably did not remember her house and thought I was dropping him with a babysitter. Who knows? Once Scotty realized I was not leaving, he settled down and played with Kerri. Her grandparents were attentive and the visit was relaxed. Kerri's family and our family are more comfortable around each other these days. I do allow some distance, time-wise, when I can. Scotty will eventually have the latitude to decide how often he sees his birth family. I do not want to over commit and create future pressure on Scotty by having too close and frequent a relationship now.

Houston usually goes with Scotty and me to visit Kerri. I want Houston and Scotty to live the open adoption journey together as brothers. This is an enormous learning opportunity for Houston, plus I do not want Scotty to feel set apart. Both boys benefit from sharing such an intimate, unique experience.

Neither Kerri nor I want Scotty to grow up feeling overly obligated to his birth family, but we also do not want him to feel abandoned. They love him. They love Houston. We *all* are committed to putting Scotty's mental health and happiness first.

The adoption journey has taught me patience, resilience, tolerance, and, above all else, how to live gratefully in the moment. I do not dare to make decisions about next year right now. I simply enjoy Scotty, Houston, my family, and friends as much as possible and make important decisions as necessary.

I am no fortune teller so there is no point in trying to tell the future. I know that someday Kerri may have children and we will have to decide what—if any—relationship Scotty and Houston will have with those children. I know that Scotty will grow into an independent thinker and may have questions, requests, and an individual perspective on his adoption and his relationship with his birth family. I want him to know that he completely belongs in the Dyer family just as Houston does. I want him to feel the unconditional connection that comes with biological relation. I do not want him to feel that any issue separates him from his brother. I pray Houston and Scotty are always close.

Permission Granted

After all I have said about how *well* Kerri and I communicate, I have to admit something. I put off telling Kerri about this book until I had almost completed it. As I approached the end of writing this book, I timidly called her to get her blessing. I would not print the book without her consent. I respect her and her family and do not want anything I write to hurt them. All along, I felt Kerri would be enthusiastic about the project, but I feared she would not want me to divulge so many intimate parts of our story. I feared she might be embarrassed. I feared she might anticipate complaints from her family. When I worked up the nerve to finally tell Kerri, I was relieved and delighted to discover she loved the book idea, and she wanted to contribute. Once again she impressed me with her unselfish nature. I explained the book's intended audience and purpose, and she said, "This could help a lot of people, Jody."

Kerri and I talked at length about how her input could help waiting parents, and we decided that a frank, one-on-one interview format would be a perfect ending for our story.

People who ask me about my relationship with Kerri often attempt to label it with a familiar association. For example, friends seek to define her role as Scotty's aunt, my friend, Scotty's big sister, or even my little sister.

I explain that her relationship with Scotty is unique, and cannot be classified by any description other than exactly what she is: Scotty's birthmother. It is special and private and should not be gawked at or reduced to common terms. Friends or family who have seen a photo of Kerri have done so only by accident. Kerri and I are not Facebook friends. I guard the Grail.

In this portion of the book, I do not imply in any way that Kerri is a prediction or reflection of the birthmother of your child, though Kerri *will* have some emotions, experiences, questions, and attitudes in common with your child's birthmother. I do believe reading Kerri's account and getting to know her through my interview may diffuse misconceptions and anxiety adoptive parents have about working with birthparents. The "interview" is really just a conversation on paper between Scotty's mother and his birthmother.

On June 19, 2012, Kerri and I met at her home, and I taped our conversation on a little cassette recorder. I asked her my questions and a few questions that she actually wrote. I am the interviewer in bold, and Kerri's responses follow my questions or comments.

I omitted some statements to protect Scotty's privacy and our current and future relationship with his birth family. My questions, sometimes lengthy, were intended to lead Kerri to elaborate on ideas and issues I thought were most important to waiting parents. I think Kerri's and my conversation will present a refreshing, candid, empathetic perspective for any reader. Through our dialogue, I want you to see *exactly* what our relationship is like now, two years after Scotty's birth.

I hope our story, our relationship, and our Scotty encourage you, inform you, inspire you, and give you calm as you wait to take your own leap of faith into the turbulent waters of adoption.

Meet Kerri

Kerri, the big question I get these days is, "What's it like now with you and the birthmom?" I think anyone who reads this will be able to tell. Are you ready?

Yeah. Sure!

Okay. Tell the story about how you found out you were pregnant.

How I found out I was pregnant?

Yes.

I was living in Pennsylvania with Bryant and some friends. One of my housemates and I were cleaning out a closet in the bathroom. She pulled out this box and it had a bunch of pregnancy tests in it from when she'd found out she was pregnant. They were all expired and she had, literally, just had a baby. What she wanted to do was pee on the stick and find out if the hormone was still in her body, if a test would still come back positive. She was like, "Well, you are not pregnant."

And I was like, "No, no, that would be impossible." I wasn't late and the only symptom I had of pregnancy—and I didn't realize it was a symptom—was I felt a little bit flu-sick and I was exhausted all the time. I would sleep for hours and hours and didn't realize why I was so tired. I was SO tired. I thought the sleeping was because of the flu and I thought I just got the flu because I was living up north and it was colder up there and it was a different environment.

So, you were the control group in the experiment.

Yes, so we both peed on sticks and set them down on the counter side-by-side. When we picked them back up, one came back positive and one came back negative. I was like, "I'm pretty sure the positive one's mine," and she said, "Maybe we got them mixed up." So, we did it again. This time, I kept my stick in the room and she took her stick downstairs. Well, her stick obviously came back negative so she came barreling up the stairs about the time I'm looking at my stick. She opened the door and saw me sitting there staring at this little stick I had just peed on. There were those two little lines. I just didn't know what to do. There's really no thought process that goes through your head when you see that, especially when it's unplanned. Like, if you are planning a pregnancy and you get the positive result thing, the little two lines, they're great. You celebrate.

Oh, it's more than great. It the most promising ink you can possibly ever see in the world.

But when you didn't think you were pregnant this was a complete, like, smack upside the head.

Shock?

Yes, it was a huge shock because I wasn't late, I didn't have any symptoms—or so I thought. There was nothing.

You just took the test as a joke.

Yeah, I didn't suspect I was pregnant and to find out I was pregnant that way was crazy. I took more pregnancy tests that day. I don't know how many I mustered up finally.

How many of them were positive?

Funny Jody. All of them. There wasn't a single negative one and I wanted at least one to be negative because I could have been like, "maybe these are all just expired and I don't have anything to worry about." Pregnancy has always been an unbelievable thing to me. I've told you several times about the shows that I've watched about how babies come to be.

Yes, how mechanically impossible it seems.

How impossible it seems and when I watch those shows and when I hear somebody talk about how it has to travel this way, it has to be a certain time, you have to be ovulating, and there are ninjas in your uterus that kill the sperm. I mean, there's so much stuff that hinders you from getting pregnant. But, then, somehow, someway, I got pregnant and it makes no sense to me.

Yes and there are people out there who desperately want to have children.

They'll do anything.

Like have sex five nights in a row, do IUIs, torture themselves with hormones. I did exactly what I was supposed to do at exactly the right times.

Yes, and nothing happened. You knew your ovulation schedule. I didn't even know my ovulation schedule. I had no idea when I ovulated. I'm aware of it now! The worst part of it is, it's so *possible* to get pregnant but somebody who is infertile takes so many pregnancy tests and they constantly get disappointment after disappointment after disappointment.

That tiny pink line would have changed my life. I would have been over the moon, but that little window on the test stick was empty, empty, empty.

Yes. That tiny pink line.

Can you see how people who are infertile become resentful?

Yeah, I can imagine. I hate the fact that there are people like you, families like you out there desperately wanting a baby and wanting to get pregnant. And I'm one of those girls who, literally, just went out and made a mistake. Well, not really a mistake. I was in a committed relationship, but you know, I didn't mean to get pregnant.

I wouldn't say you were careless. You just did something that lots of other people do, and, uh-oh! Do you think that people in general assume that birthmothers are ignorant when it comes to birth control? That they look down on you and judge, "Why would you get in that situation?" I mean, regarding birth control, you are completely informed and you just did what was right for you.

You can't be uninformed about birth control in this day and age because you get an education about it in school and on TV.

I know! We've got the TV on to watch "Teen Mom" right now and a birth control ad *just* came on. So far we've seen commercials that are anti-drug, anti-texting, anti-unprotected sex.

And Green Dot credit cards! It wasn't that I was careless. We used a method—not the greatest method in the world—but we used birth control. And we were in a committed relationship for over two years.

Really, each birthmother's situation is unique. What myths do you think there are about birthmothers?

We are crackheads! I hear we are all drug addicts and meth-heads and prostitutes and we don't know who the baby daddy is. We're all terrible people and there's no way we could ever parent. And, we don't want children. We don't love the babies and we don't want children ever.

What would you say to birthmothers considering adoption?

Make sure it's what you want because once you get into it, and you pick a family, it's an overwhelming process. You've got to be strong to do it. Once you pick that family, it's not just about you anymore. I wouldn't blame somebody if she backed out, but if she does, there's a whole other family that she's hurting. Oh, here come Catelynn and Tyler on "Teen Mom." They are celebrating Carly's birthday.

Let's stop and watch. (*We pause to see Catelynn, Tyler, Brandon, Theresa, and Carly reunite on "Teen Mom."*)

Okay, we checked on Catelynn and Tyler. So, let's go back. You were in the bathroom and saw two pink lines, and thought, "Oh, no." What was the first thing you did?

The first thing I did was take more tests, hoping one would turn out negative since they were expired or because some crazy hormone was in my body making me seem pregnant. In my head, that's what I thought. But, the day went on, and it was time for Bryant to get off work.

So, you didn't call him? You were just reeling and dealing with it by yourself? When you told him, what did you all do?

He kind of thought like I did, that the tests may be bad, so he wanted to get a new one and take it in the morning. So we bought the new test and brought it home. He played Call of Duty all night and I sat there on his laptop looking up symptoms and everything, still trying to find a diagnosis saying I wasn't pregnant. We barely slept that night. I woke up the next morning and took the test. We laid the pregnancy test face down on the dresser. We sat on the edge of the bed. We waited the full five minutes because we didn't want to mess up.

How did those five minutes feel?

That was like an eternity. It really was. You know, I went through being pregnant for nine months but that five minutes waiting for that test to come back felt longer than my entire pregnancy. It was a massive amount of time.

It was a fifty-fifty situation.

Yeah, well, I didn't want to look at the test because I knew.

At that point, I had slept on it and I was like, *I'm pregnant, there's no other way, there's no other explanation for all those tests to come back positive. No way.* I made Bryant look at the stick. He picked it up, turned it over, and turned to me with the dumbest look on his face. I KNOW he's smarter than this, but he looked at me and said, "Hey, uh, babe, what do TWO lines mean?"

He didn't even know what to look for? (laughing)

I said, "Bryant, I'm pregnant." He stayed home from work that day and we started looking at places I could go to to get my official pregnancy test, my first ultrasound. I went to a little clinic in downtown Reading. It was a nice little place. We went with our good friend and she was great through the whole thing. She was the only person who knew about the pregnancy, except for our roommate. We hadn't told anybody yet. I hadn't called any of my family; I hadn't called any of my friends. I hadn't done anything.

Why not?

I think I wanted to make sure. I wanted to physically see that there was a baby in my uterus before I called anyone. When we went in there, Bryant sat down and I went back in the back and they gave me the pregnancy test and it came back positive. Well, you know what it looks like, you have it. It was a little bitty tiny stick.

Yeah, you gave me the *actual* test stick that you took in the clinic.

I kept it. It was just one of those things I didn't get rid of. Kind of weird I guess.

I'm glad, Kerri. It means a lot to me that you gave me that test. I mean, I know you tee-teed on it. But, in the end, I got to experience the two pink lines. The sixty-sixth test I looked at was POSITIVE!

I know! Well, we went back to the ultrasound room. It was overwhelming because they lay you out on this table and they put this tarp over you and you don't have any pants on and it's a really weird place to be.

I was back there by myself at first and they said Bryant could come back there later after the technician made sure everything was okay and there was a baby in there. She first tried to get a picture on my stomach like a normal ultrasound but she couldn't. So she had to use that big long stick thing and the only thing I vividly remember is that she put a condom on it. I looked at the ultrasound technician as she was doing it and said, "Well, obviously it's a little late for that!" I cracked up the ultrasound tech and the doctor that was back there. When they first pulled up the baby on the screen, he looked like a peanut.

So, when was this? August?

No, September. I got pregnant in August. I was actually six weeks pregnant when I found out. I hadn't missed a period or anything. I was actually on schedule with everything, which I've heard that some people do. So the ultrasound tech, when she pulled it up, this little peanut is wiggling on a screen and she says, "There's your baby. This is going to be its head, this is its body. It doesn't really have limbs yet, well it does, they are beginning but you can't see them." So, it just kind of wiggles around and I'm looking at it.

So, she said Bryant could come back there so the doctor went and got him. Bryant stood behind me at the head of the bed. He looked at the screen and said, "Where's the baby?" and I said, "It's right there. Do you see that little thing right there?" and he said, "That doesn't look like a baby. It looks like a peanut." I was like, "They don't really look like babies when they first start out. They look like weird little alien creatures."

The alien look resurfaces in middle school.

Yeah! It was really weird being in that ultrasound room. From that point on, it was real. I still have the picture.

Do you think it felt more real because you saw that little person wiggling around?

It was real as soon as I saw. With the stick tests, it was a chemical thing. It wasn't until I saw physically my little peanut baby that it sunk in. I was like, *Holy crap, in nine months there's going to be another human being on this planet and it's going to be because of me. And it's in there and there's something growing inside me. It's like a parasite.*

Ha! It's a parasite forever, even when it's out! It takes everything you've got.

They are even parasites when they are eighteen and you think they're gone. They come back! For me, that was what I kind of thought, like, *There is this thing inside of me and it's eating my food and it's making me exhausted, and making me feel like I have the flu.*

So, were you at a free health clinic?

It was a free health clinic.

Thank God there are places like that Kerri.

I know. Where else was I going to go? We didn't have insurance. I had to get a positive pregnancy test from a clinic or the health department before I could apply for pregnancy insurance. Some states offer free pregnancy insurance for some people, which is the most useful thing in the world because when you are pregnant and very low income like me, you don't have the ability to be like, "Well, I'm pregnant so I'll just go buy some insurance."

You know, for all those years, I carried maternity coverage. It was fifty to one hundred dollars a month. All those years I paid that. What a waste.

I know. Having the free pregnancy insurance and clinics are extremely important. When I hear people say, "Why do we need places like that?" I tell them that people like me who are very low income don't have insurance. We have no other way.

I know you weren't working then but you do typically work. A lot of people don't have insurance. Jeff went without it for three years when he was self-employed. Some people don't even realize they have access to help. You are smart and resourceful so you found out what you needed and how to get it.

The best thing to do if you are in an unplanned pregnancy is literally, to get on Google, and type in "pregnancy options." If you are in that area, it will give you clinics you can go to. At the clinics, it doesn't matter which situation you choose. If you choose adoption, abortion, parenting, everything you need as far as information goes is there.

There are organizations out there that want to see healthy babies come into the world. They will take care of the mother.

Yes, and there are so many more options out there. Like, my mom told me when she got pregnant with me, there weren't clinics like that. The pre-natal vitamins that she took were like huge horse pills and now there are granola bars.

Even Jeff's birthmother had no pre-natal care. I think it was more out of shame. Or denial maybe. It was 1963.

Yeah, pregnancy is such an important and different topic now.

I want to know about what was going on at that point in your relationship with Bryant. Some girls say that's when birthfathers fold or propose. Why didn't you get married?

We talked about marriage then but we knew we were not ready for that.

You all were pretty young.

He was twenty.

So you both turned twenty-one during the pregnancy?

Yes. His twenty-first birthday was a lot different than mine!

Why did you choose adoption?

In the situation I was in it was really the best. I wasn't completely ready to be a mom.

Why not?

Well, I was too young. I had a lot of stuff I still wanted to do. I'm not going to say I was super immature because I was a lot more mature than most people my age. I wasn't in the right situation. I lived in a room that was so tiny. We had room for a bed, a dresser, and a closet. That was all the room we had. There was no room for a baby in that situation. Where would we put a bed? Where would we put a changing table? How would we get diapers? He was the only one working. It was not a good situation. We shared a house with four other people and there was already another newborn baby living there.

So, it was a little chaotic?

It was more than a little chaotic. It was a constant mess. The baby was about two months old when I found out I was pregnant. I took care of him a lot.

So you knew what it was like to have a newborn.

Oh, yeah, I knew what it was like. He was under a bili-light because he had jaundice. Sometimes he was sick and I was the only one home. So I had to watch the baby. So, for the first two months of his life, I was taking care of him a lot. At two in the morning, he would scream and cry and I would get up to help him. So I knew exactly, if I kept the baby, what I would be getting myself into. There was no guarantee my baby would have jaundice but I knew he was going to wake up and cry. After seeing that, I knew I wasn't ready.

And if I stayed in that situation, during the pregnancy, I would be taking care of myself while I was pregnant and I'd also be taking care of their baby, and then when I had my baby, I'd be taking care of their baby *and* my baby. It wasn't really something I wanted to do. Not at all.

So, when I found out I was pregnant, the very next day is when we made the adoption plan. I didn't want to have an abortion. I respect a woman's right to choose what she does with her body, but I know the statistics, and I know how many people are out there waiting for a baby.

You know that now, but did you know that then?

I knew a little bit about it.

When you were younger, before you got pregnant, did you know anyone who had abortions?

I did. My friend got an abortion. Her reason was she was raised in a [very religious] household and if her family had found out she was pregnant it would have been very bad.

I think that in your generation, the social current pushes toward single parenting or abortion.

Yeah, it does.

Adoption is this unknown option or afterthought. It's not in the forefront.

No, adoption is not really in the forefront. Girls get pregnant, and they think they have two options: abort it or raise it.

Not a lot of people understand that there is that middle option. You don't have to raise your child and you don't have to kill it, either.

I guess, for many women, it seems like the quick easy thing to do. Your problem is solved. You go on with life. It's sad.

There's no way, no way, I could have lived with myself the rest of my life if I'd had an abortion. If I had done it, I would have never been the same. I might never have children because I might feel so guilty about what I did. For me, it wasn't worth it. There are other damages it can do to your body.

Some girls in a crisis don't fully understand all the ramifications.

No, they may think abortion is always safe, nothing can go wrong with it, it's not going to cause fertility problems later in life, and you're not going to have any guilt about it. They think it's a quick in and out, doctor takes care of it, and you leave.

That's what some believe. And some feel like they have no other solution, no "choice." But you faced all the discomfort and stress of pregnancy for nine months, knowing the whole time you were not going to parent the baby.

Yes. I enjoyed my pregnancy. I loved being pregnant. There was something about being fat and huge. It was fun being pregnant. I could set a cereal bowl on my stomach.

Don't you think food tastes better when you are pregnant?

YES! Food tastes a lot better, except for the beginning of your pregnancy when you can't eat anything because you are sick. Other than that, I could handle being pregnant for nine months. Some people just don't have that option.

To some girls, nine months seems like an impossible amount of time. And, they have no support. You had a supportive birthfather. Bryant backed your adoption decision immediately, right?

~ 234 ~

Yes, he did. Obviously, Bryant and I no longer have a relationship. With our personal situations we were going through we could no longer continue as a couple. But, as Scotty's birthfather, throughout the pregnancy, even though our relationship suffered a lot, he never stopped supporting me. He called after every doctor's appointment. He made sure I was doing okay.

I think there's a lot of mutual respect. That's what I've seen between you two.

Yes, during the first part of the pregnancy we actually got closer.

But you moved.

Yes, after I moved to Tennessee, we split.

Why did you move to Tennessee?

Well, I wasn't actually planning on moving back to Tennessee. I came down here for my birthday. My relationship with my family was very strained at the time because they did not approve of me being in Pennsylvania. They did not approve of Bryant. They did not like him. They have the idea that because I was born in Tennessee the rest of my life should be spent in Tennessee and I shouldn't have left. They think there is nothing better than Tennessee. It's the greatest state on the planet.

It's the greenest!

It *is* the greenest. It's a very awesome state. I'm not mad at Pennsylvania, though.

So they were mad and your relationship was strained. When you got to Tennessee, was it hard to tell your family you were pregnant?

Yes, actually, I told friends before I told family.

You know, even though my family was supportive, my friends talked and asked about the adoption more openly. And they were less judgmental. But, they also didn't have as much at stake either. I do think it's harder to tell family. Maybe it's harder because you need their support and fear their reactions.

I agree. I told my good friend here in Tennessee and she was unbelievable.

She was the one who went to lunch with us at Panera.

She's the one who went to lunch with us at Panera. She was at the hospital. She was an amazing support and she was with me pretty much every day. She took me out. We spent a lot of time together so I wasn't sitting at home by myself when I was pregnant. When you are in a situation where you are doing an adoption, you try not to bond with the baby like a normal mother does. I had to stay busy. When you are pregnant, and you are becoming a mother, and you are going to parent, it is a different feeling. This is your child and you are so excited and you can't wait to see it and you are going to name it and raise it.

And you can make plans.

You can bond.

At the same time, as the adoptive parent, you are kind of wondering, *Am I ever going to get a baby?* **Let's talk about bonding. You named him London. Why did you do that?**

For me it was easier. I didn't want a baby inside me that didn't have a name. I needed it to have a name. I think I called him Peanut until I found out what he was. I was always excited about ultrasounds and things like that. Even though I was not going to keep my baby afterwards, it was still awesome. A life was growing inside of me. It was a really interesting process.

Did you feel more like a babysitter than a mother?

Not really.

Let's talk about what happened once you decided adoption was the best choice for you.

Well, I went to the little clinic and talked to people there. They gave me little brochures and asked me what I was going to do.

And you said you could not parent this child.

Yeah. So the clinic gave us a bunch of brochures. They gave me brochures for abortion and adoption. The abortion brochures were really nice. They were pretty and laminated and had pictures of happy women and stuff, which is kind of sickening to me because the women on the covers were running through fields of flowers and holding streamers.

They are FREE!

Right, so that's really crazy. The adoption brochures, a lot of them, were printed out on typing paper and just folded to make them look like brochures and they were in all black ink.

They had pictures of Asian kids and Ethiopian kids and stuff. I have no problem with international adoption; I think it's great, but they didn't look relevant to Bryant and me and our baby. Bethany, their brochure was a lot different. It was laminated, it was pretty, and it was a really nice little brochure. It looked more professional.

It showed you more respect.

Yes. It actually had people on it who looked like they were from here. Like, they talked about international adoption but they talked about domestic adoption a lot. Like, they had a nice couple on the front and a not obviously foreign baby. It spoke to me more. That's the reason I chose Bethany. They looked like they knew what they were doing.

Maybe the adoption agencies, compared to abortion clinics, just cut costs on marketing to spend money on reaching out to people.

Yeah, and abortion costs money to do. You have to pay to get an abortion so maybe the abortion clinics have more money to throw into advertising. Adoption agencies work on donations.

They have donors and fundraisers. Plus, adoptive parents pay placement and home study fees.

Yeah, the birthparents don't pay. I guess adoption agencies don't have a lot of money to throw into brochures and stuff because they are taking care of birthparents and waiting parents.

Bethany is just really good at what they do.

They *are* good.

What were your views on adoption before?

My view on adoption before was the same as most people's. It's a closed situation. You have the baby, you pop it out, you hand it over, and that's it. You don't see it anymore.

Did you know a lot about adoption?

No, I saw it on TV.

Yeah, I was advised not to watch some fictional adoption movies. They show the worst possible scenarios sometimes.

Yes, don't watch if you're a birthmother either. I'm not telling you *not* to watch [a certain channel]. It's quality TV.

Some movies make us all look a little crazy. My being crazy has nothing to do with the fact that I'm infertile!

Ha! Yeah! The birthmothers are portrayed as drug addicts and prostitutes.

We steal babies from the hospital.

Yeah, you run away with them!

We have fake nurse uniforms so we can slide in and out inconspicuously.

You should have come to the hospital in a fake nurse's costume!

Ha! I'm sure I looked like a psycho when I was there. I was out of my mind.

You first met with a Bethany social worker in Pennsylvania?

I met with an adoption worker in Pennsylvania, and she was AWESOME! She was so nice. I cannot remember her name. She was pregnant.

Was that weird?

I thought it was because I was like, how are you going to be a birthmother counselor when you're pregnant? She said it was a lot harder than people think. She was heavily pregnant.

Heavily pregnant?

Yeah. You know those plastic things that you put under your desk so your chair can roll around? She had that down. I said, "What are you going to do when you have your baby? Are you going to be here for us?" She said "Well, I'll take my maternity leave but that's it. That's why I have this plastic down here in case my water breaks while I'm at work. We can wipe it up really quickly." She was a really funny lady and I really liked her. Bethany, as soon as I went in, was nothing like I had expected it to be. I thought adoption was like, you're pregnant, you sign this paper, and they pick out a family for you and say, "Alright, see you in nine months."

With adoption, you had a lot more choices than you expected.

Absolutely, a lot more choices.

You had all the say.

I hate to say it, but when you go into the adoption situation with an agency like Bethany, the entire world revolves around you, the birthmother. Like, you get healthcare. You get to pick your family, they help you with clothes, they help you with rent, cell phones, if you need rides to the doctor, if you need help getting insurance, prenatal vitamins, they help you. When I went into the adoption situation, I thought everything revolved around the parents that were going to adopt but it really doesn't. They really care about birthmothers.

Because Kerri, even though so many babies are born in crisis situations, relatively few babies are given up for adoption. And there are *so many* people trying to adopt. Birthparents really do have control. Jeff and I felt competitive, which is absurd. My cousin looked at the online profiles on the Bethany website and was sizing up my competition. She said, "Okay, those people have got nothing on you and Jeff. They don't even have flowers in their yard."

It's the Battle Royale. Adoption agencies should have a scoreboard. Just kidding.

Why did you *stay* down here in Tennessee?

I was getting really bad night nausea. I could not handle another plane ride. I was supposed to only stay with my family for those three weeks around my birthday, but I needed their help. Then the plan was I'd just stay down here until the pregnancy was done. I was going to do all the adoption stuff while I was down here but still use the Pennsylvania Bethany. I would still pick a family from up there and they would come down and get the baby. I was going to go back to Pennsylvania after everything was over.

Well, my relationship with Bryant started getting really strained and the house we were living in—I absolutely hated the conditions. It was nothing against Bryant.

It would be hard to be pregnant and uncomfortable. Plus, that other baby was there.

Yeah and the baby was there. There was no way I could have done it. It was too much. I made the decision to stay in Tennessee for my pregnancy and I lived with my mother.

And she helped you?

She helped me a lot. She kept me fed and gave me a place to live. She wasn't very supportive of my adoption decision. She fought it.

What did she say when you told her you were pregnant?

Oh, God, she started talking about nurseries and what we were going to do. I told her, "Mom, I'm not really sure I'm going to parent" and she was like, "Well, you are not getting an abortion." I said, "No, I'm not getting an abortion. I'm looking at adoption." And she said, "That means you'll never see the baby again." My mom had the same views on adoption that I'd had. So, that was very difficult. I'm an extremely stubborn person. I'm pretty sure that Scotty is going to have that trait. Everybody in my family is stubborn and Bryant is stubborn. We are set in our ways. There's nothing you can do to change that.

I've seen some stubbornness in little Scotty, for sure. So she was mad. Mad hurt? Mad at you?

I think it was a combination of everything. She was excited because she enjoys babies. Oh, God, this book is going to be all about my mom. She's going to kill me! I know she's going to read it.

No, we'll be very respectful toward her. We don't want her mad at us! I like Lynn.

Ha! We'll end up in night court.

What about your father?

My dad was very supportive. I did not tell my dad I was pregnant; I made my mom do it. What's funny is the day before I left for Pennsylvania the last time, my dad told me, "You know what's gonna happen, right?"

I was like, "What?"

He was like, "You're gonna go up there and you're gonna get pregnant," and I did NOT want my dad to be right. Well, I went up there and I got pregnant and my dad was right. I know that the adoption wasn't what he wanted me to do but my dad was supportive. But my mom and my grandfather didn't like the adoption.

Did your grandfather know early on that you had decided on adoption?

Yes, but we kept him as little informed as possible. I don't think it sank in until afterwards.

Your grandfather is very loving and generous and offered to help you with the baby. A lot of girls would say "okay" and keep the baby.

How did you deal with family members' arguments?

I wasn't ready. I knew what I needed to do. When I'm ready, I'll know. I want to be married, in a stable relationship, married for at least a year, maybe two, before I even consider having children. A lot of people would have taken that offer and run.

***Most* girls would. But you wanted Scotty to have a better upbringing.**

I wanted him to have two parents.

At the same time in the same place.

Yes! Two parents at the same time. I didn't want him to have to deal with the custody thing. *I* didn't want to deal with any of that. I didn't want to have to say, "Well son, I live in Tennessee and your father lives in Pennsylvania." For me, adoption was just a much better option.

Really, what you gave him is what you want to provide for your child when you are ready.

Yes, exactly. That's what I wanted. He has parents. Well, he has two sets of parents. He has me and Bryant and he has Jody and Jeff. You're mommy and daddy and we're whatever we're going to be whenever he figures it out.

I guess he'll call you Kerri and Bryant.

Yep, that's who we are.

So, at Bethany you learned about *open* adoption and what that was. How did that make you feel?

I was excited because I knew that I wasn't the kind of person who could just give my baby away and never see it again.

One time you told me that that could have been a deal-breaker.

Yeah, a closed adoption could have been a deal-breaker for me.

Some birthparents and adoptive parents choose closed adoption. There's no right or wrong, good or bad way.

Yes, that's true. You just have to do what makes you comfortable.

Why would closed adoption be wrong for *you*?

There's no way I could have done it. I would go crazy. I would have been like, *Where is he, what's he doing, what's he look like, is he okay, what's going on with him?*

So, no mystery.

No mystery. No black hole.

I guess it depends on personalities. That's one way we are alike. We are both very open people. So, when you learned about open adoption, I guess you found relief because then you knew you could be part of his future.

Yeah, and once you figure out what kind of adoption you want to do, you get to the point where you can pick out a family. You usually pick a family later but I picked a family right after I found out I was having a boy.

Why did you pick a family so early in your pregnancy?

I knew that was my way of committing. When I chose a family and I saw them and met them and knew that these were the people who would have my child, that was the lock and key on me doing it. I knew that if I had somebody else depending on me, there's no way I could disappointment them. There is no way I could disappoint somebody like that.

You *are* very considerate, even with little things. I write in the book about how you were always on time every time we met. That put me at ease like you wouldn't believe.

I'm usually thirty minutes early for everything I do unless I'm going somewhere like a party. Then I'm thirty minutes fashionably late.

When you got to pick a family, what were you looking for? Did you want someone who was like you?

Sort of. I was looking for someone really down to earth. There were certain things I wanted. It would have been nice to have someone who was super rich and loaded and had fifteen cars.

We would be if we hadn't spent all our money on fertility treatments!

Yeah! Picking is weird. I wanted somebody normal, which is weird, because a lot of people would say "I want my baby to go to some rich family" so he could go to Ivy League schools and stuff. Some privileged kids don't end up that well and I wanted my baby to know that you have to work for what you get, that there's not an easy way out. I was looking for a family that was like me, had some of the same interests as me. Which is funny because you guys do have some of the same interests as me.

But you guys are so different from me, too. Houston was all about swimming and baseball. The baby's father and I are the furthest thing from athletic. I like baseball, I watch it. But, throw a baseball at me and I'm more than likely going to duck and run away. You guys are very sports oriented. Scotty has a background that is not sports oriented at all. There was another family that I liked before I got to your profile. I really liked them. They had three other kids, a vacation home, and they were LOADED. Their picture profile book looked like it was put together by a professional photographer. It was crazy good.

Why didn't you pick them?

Because I wanted my son to be raised in a more normal situation. I wanted my son to have siblings, but I didn't want him to have four or five of them. I would feel like if there was one or two siblings, that's different, but it was like…

Too much?

Yes. I've always seen those movies where kids grow up real privileged and turn out conceited. I wanted my son to have a real down to earth family, not really a "we have five vacation homes and we summer in London and all" one.

We go to Sevierville sometimes.

Yeah, and one thing I liked about your profile *was* the farm.

We were there yesterday. I wish you could have seen Scotty. He was running full speed for the barn. He was flying and yelling "Grandmama, Grandmama!" I can't wait to see him ride his Big Wheel down her gravel driveway like Houston used to do.

Ha! I was riding a Big Wheel the other day. It was fun! Going through those profiles was so overwhelming.

Describe that scene. That's something that adoptive parents never see. So let's look behind the curtain. In your case, your mom Lynn was with you. So Lauren and Mark gave you profiles to read?

I had a lot of profiles I could go through. It was really sad because, going through those profiles, I wanted to pick everybody. Everybody wanted a baby and I understood that.

I guess the reverse situation would be really hard, too. What if Jeff and I had to look through a catalog of babies? My cousin David played basketball overseas and visited an orphanage and said it just about killed him.

Yes. And you have to pick one. I was like, you know, H*oly crap, what do I do? I have all these families and they all want babies and I want to give them all babies but I can't give all of them babies. How do I do this?*

That's a good point that you make, Kerri. Birthparents sympathize with adoptive families.

Yes, we do.

You also understand many of us have suffered loss and we are sad.

Yeah, we're in two different situations but we're melded into one.

How did you narrow it down? Was it based on looks? Ha!

NO. Well, it wasn't *always* based on looks. Ha! One other couple I was looking at were gamers and Bryant is really into video games. He was so pumped up about a video gaming family.

Houston has a Wii. I don't know how to set it up, though.

It's not hard Jody. You just have to match up the red to the red and the white to the white.

When you had that stack, did you sort-of label the profiles like 'too preppy, too religious, too old...?' Did you look at every one?

I looked at every one. I flipped through the pages. I read all the birthparent letters. Those were the first things I actually read.

Did you care about age? My mother-in-law was worried Jeff was too old to get a baby. I mean, Jeff's older than your mother.

A little bit. Age was a little bit of a concern because I didn't want to pick somebody too old because maybe they'd die before my baby was eighteen. That would blow. When I picked you guys, there were so many similarities. Your wedding anniversary is Bryant's birthday. You guys have a Yorkie and I love Yorkies. Jeff being adopted was a huge thing for me. Knowing that my son was going to grow up in a family that already had adoption in their family was great, especially since the *father* was adopted. I knew Jeff could help counsel my son through whatever he would go through. *He's* been through it.

So if my son comes up to Jeff one day when he's eleven or twelve and he's starting to really understand what happened, especially with the open adoption because Scotty's going to know his whole life, Jeff is there. If he has any questions I know for a fact he can call me, but if he wants to talk to Jeff about what he's feeling, Jeff could be the first person he goes to and Jeff will help him.

I agree. I see some insecurity in Jeff sometimes. That's normal. Think about things you hear like 'blood is thicker than water' or 'birthright' or 'it's in his blood.' You never know when Scotty's a teenager what he'll be thinking.

What would you say to families who are writing "Dear Birthparent" letters and creating profiles right now?

I think the best advice, coming from a birthmother, that I can give to adoptive families who are making their profiles is just be as real as possible. Don't try to make it all Hollywood and pretty. We know that life isn't perfect. Everybody has their skeletons in the closet or weird little quirks or habits. Just be as honest as possible. Be yourself, because that's what we're looking for, not people who are trying to be something else.

You want to know EXACTLY who is getting your baby. Did anything in those profiles turn you off?

Just the people who seemed too good to be true. Like the ones whose profiles looked like they were done by a Hollywood director and were too perfect. We're looking for somebody that's real. We're not looking for the perfect family because there's no such thing as the perfect family. Every family has their things.

What about Houston's little paragraph?

About teaching him to swim? That was so great. I loved the fact that Houston was involved. The other families I looked at who had kids, they didn't really let them add anything. They were like, "We have four kids, their names and ages, etcetera."

Houston was highly engaged and I got criticized for that. I got questions like, "Are you sure you should be telling him so much?" Houston absolutely wanted a sibling. I wrote down word-for-word exactly what he said to write. What's funny is he couldn't even read when he promised to teach the baby to read.

Going through the profiles was very overwhelming. I described it to a friend of mine who was wondering what it was like. I told her it's kind of like how they say when you're looking for a wedding dress and you put "the one" on, you just know. That's kind of how it is with a family. There's a connection before you even meet them.

I had a "no" stack. I had a "maybe" stack. The "yes" stack was just your profile. That was the only one in there. The "no" stack I pushed aside and they took them away. I went to my "maybe" stack for my second choice. I didn't even put my second choice on top of your profile. It was a really interesting process.

So then we met.

Yeah, then we met.

Do you remember seeing me in the hallway?

I do. I do remember seeing you. It was really funny because I wasn't sure that that was you.

Well, my hair was a different color in every picture of the profile book.

Yeah, your hair WAS a different color. I remember going in and I was really excited. There's a bowl of candy in the hallway and I was pregnant and I really wanted some candy so what I was actually doing was peeking around the corner to see what kind of candy was in that bowl. Sometimes they have these little banana Tootsie Rolls and those things were the bomb when I was pregnant. So I was peaking around and I looked up and there you were.

For a second I was like, *Wow, is that her?* and I ducked my head back really quickly. It was really interesting seeing you. I saw Mark standing next to you and I thought, *That's got to be her.* Of course, when we walked down the hallway to go to the room where we would meet you guys, I was throwing candy in my purse. You didn't see it but there was a gob of candy in my purse that day.

It's weird. I remember getting up that morning and going through everything to try to figure out what to wear and I wore a black turtleneck.

So you worried about what you were going to wear?

Yeah. I wanted to cover up my tattoos. I didn't want you to see them all the way.

I thought about what I was going to wear, too. I worried you would get the wrong impression. I wanted to look like a mother but not a dud. Well, women dress for other women.

They do! The problem with being pregnant is you are huge.

You were not huge. At that point you were only five months pregnant. I'm sure I outweighed you!

I had some rounding going on. And, I got bigger and bigger. At that time, I was just to the point where you could tell I was pregnant. You know once you go through pregnancy you don't know what your body looks like anymore. I had just put the stretchy band in my pants.

When we walked in there, could you tell I was nervous?

Yeah, but I was nervous, too.

Why were you nervous? You had all the power.

I was afraid you would think differently of me because I had my lip pierced, I had a tongue ring, I had tattoos. I didn't think I was the norm of what a birthmother should look like. And, of course, I'm a very outspoken person. I'm very loud, I'm very talkative, and I'm very "out there." I figured you guys would be very reserved and quiet.

Jeff was quiet.

The one thing I've learned about Jeff is that he's typically quiet.

He's got a great personality but, in a situation like that, if he's not sure, he's just not going to say anything. That whole experience was overwhelming for him, Kerri.

Meeting you guys was great. We had a great conversation. I told you all about where I was in my pregnancy.

Some birthmothers choose not to meet the adoptive parents. Would you encourage birthmothers to try to meet the families, even if the adoption isn't going to be open or *as* open as ours?

Yes, I would, very much. Because, when you meet the family, it sets your decision [in place] a lot more. It makes the decision a lot easier because now you have two people that you don't really want to let down.

And some birthparents just want a completely closed adoption. Which is fine and understandable.

Yeah, they don't want to know anything about it and don't want the adoptive parents to know anything about them.

So, did you feel like you were the interviewer or the interviewee? We felt like we were being interviewed. Did you feel like we were watching you, judging you?

I knew you guys wouldn't judge me. From your profile and how you guys seemed in that, I knew you guys would be good. And when we met, you guys seemed so interested in everything I said, the whole time. I didn't want to interview anybody else. I was pretty much set that you guys were the family. Once I left that day, it was solid. I wanted to know more about you guys, but before you agreed to adopt my son, I wanted you to know who I was.

You said something to me after lunch at Calhoun's one time. I said, "I like you Kerri" and you said, "Good, cause he's going to be a little me!"

He might wake up one day and say, "Mom, I want a tattoo!"

Oh, Lord!

He is going to be a lot like me. He's got my DNA. It's interesting to see nature versus nurture.

You know what's funny? He's stubborn, he's friendly, and he loves mango and bananas like you do, but he is obsessed with sports. He won't let me change the TV off the Golf Channel and he's two years old! He mimics the catcher on the baseball team. He has Houston's little free throw warm-up routine down. That's all Houston's influence.

That's the nurture part.

So we got along great. We went to lunch and got to know each other. Do you think that helped you?

That helped a lot. When you get to know the person who is going to raise your child it is easier to be okay with giving him up to her.

Were you nervous when we went to lunch? I was.

For the first few times, yes. After a while, I just thought, *Jody's going to raise my child.*

I would say to birthparents, if they get to know the adoptive families, any reassurance they can give is really sweet.

Yes, because these people are waiting for your baby and you have all the power to say "No."

It's a scary place to be. Plus, we were off the list. When you read this memoir, I don't want you to think I didn't trust you. But you are going to see my fear. The fear is completely normal. The threat is real. Speaking of, let's talk about the hospital. How would you describe the hospital experience from your perspective?

My hospital experience was crazy! Do you remember how many people I had in my room?

Yes. Just before you had Scotty, EVERYBODY showed up. So Jeff and I kind of hid out.

Yeah, which is not what I wanted.

I know. We just did that out of respect for them and to make things easier on you.

Honestly, I would have been happy keeping it down to just like you and Jeff, my mom, and [my friends]. My friends were extremely supportive. My mom was having a hard time. It was exhausting because I was in labor for twelve hours. We went in at 6:00 in the morning. They broke my water at 7:00 a.m., and I didn't have him until 7:21 p.m. that night. I went through all the labor. The worst thing I can tell anybody about the hospital experience as the birthmother is that my biggest problem was that I was so hungry. You and Jeff didn't eat in front of me, which was great. I don't even think you guys ate until after the baby was born.

I lost four pounds in the hospital.

But my mom and [my friends] and everybody else who was there brought in like Wendy's and Taco Bell and were eating it and I was like, "I'M SO HUNGRY!"

I remembered being in labor with Houston and starving, so I could sympathize. I felt sorry for you.

With some people there was no consideration. I was thinking, *I'm in freaking labor here. I'm not really doing okay.*

***And* you were giving the baby away.**

Yeah, that's why my doctor cleared everybody out of my room at one point. And, it was an extremely stressful labor because it was so long.

At least you had an epidural.

Yeah, I wasn't in pain. Until the C-section. Once we knew the C-section was coming, I had a panic attack and I got sick. I'm going to tell this to every single person, adoptive mothers, birthmothers, anyone that will have children. If you are in the hospital and you get to eat something, make sure it's the banana popsicles because they taste exactly the same coming up as they do going down. It's good advice because if you're going to get sick, stick with the banana popsicles. It's a little bit spicier coming back up, though.

Was your mother still hoping you'd change your mind?

Yes.

She was, and is, always really sweet to me. You understand that she suffered a loss, too?

Yes. I do. In the delivery room I remember flashes of things because I was so doped up. I wanted an epidural because there was no way I was doing it naturally but I wanted to do vaginal delivery.

I wanted the birth to be as natural and normal as possible. Being back in that operating room, especially when you are doing adoption, you know that you are doing all this basically for nothing. I mean, not for *nothing*.

I understand what you are saying. You are going home fat, cut up, in pain, worn out, and without a baby.

Yeah, exactly, so you are doing all this for not really anything for yourself. I mean, you get to satisfy another couple and give them a baby and that is the ultimate gift. But then, your body has to suffer for it a lot.

So I was back in the C-section room and they strapped my arms down and this big blue thing was in front of me and I couldn't see anything going on. I was lying on my back, big and pregnant. I know a lot of people who have been pregnant understand this; when you are pregnant, lying on your back is the most uncomfortable thing. I was suffering because he was so low and he was trying to come out and he got stuck. They did the C-section. He finally came out. My mom immediately left me because they put Scotty on one of those table things. She was over there with the baby. My friend was with me while they were taking out whatever the heck they have to take out and sewing me back up and all that stuff. They did that and I couldn't see the baby. He was on a table and there were people in front of me so I couldn't see him.

They didn't hold him up and show him to you?

No. They did not hold him up.

Did they ask you if you wanted to see the baby? Because I know they put him in the bed with you eventually.

When they got me all sewn up, they took my epidural out and put me on another bed. When they put me on another bed, the first thing of Scotty I saw was purple feet up in the air. I was looking over and he wasn't really crying. He was just kind of whining. There wasn't a huge cry. I thought he would belt it out. He was my kid so I figured he'd have a really loud voice but he was very quiet. He was real chilled out.

He still is, most of the time, except when he's stubborn.

The nurse that was there—she was great—she asked, "Do you want us to carry the baby or do you want to hold the baby when you go out?"

I said, "I want to see him." I was really messed up. I started shaking. I wasn't cold. I was actually burning up. People were throwing blankets on me. So, she handed Scotty to me. He was tucked up right here under my arm. I don't remember the ride back. I don't think it was because I was all messed up. I think I don't remember it because, as soon as they put him in my arms, I was *focused*. His eyes were wide open and he was staring. I stared at him. I was thinking, *Did I make that? Is that me right there?* Because he looked like me. That was the weirdest thing for me. That was overwhelming. He'd always been this little sea monkey that lived in my belly and I'd never seen his face before. I didn't get to have one of those 3D ultrasounds. His face was a whole other different experience.

Did you love him immediately?

Oh yeah. The weird thing was, even though I had that huge moment, I was still not questioning what I wanted to do.

Would there have been a difference if Bryant had been there?

I know that Bryant would have helped. It would not have been my mom in that room. My friend wouldn't have been in there either. It probably would have been me, Bryant, and you.

I don't want readers to think he didn't care.

Oh, no, that poor kid. He cared. When I talked to Bryant's friend a few weeks later, he said that Bryant sat on the porch and chain-smoked all night.

It had to be awful for him. I know he would have been there if he could have been.

Yes.

Alright, so then everybody kind of pounced on you. Your family.

When I made my birth plan, I had a plan. It was written down. My birth plan blew all to Hell.

That's normal in any pregnancy. These women plan water and home births and end up at the medical center. But, for you, it was important that it went right.

Yeah, I didn't want my family to be the first ones to see the baby. I wanted you to be the first one back there. But, when I got out of the delivery room, I was messed up. Typically, I can pretty much keep my family at bay.

You were completely vulnerable.

Yeah, I was really vulnerable. I don't even know what drugs they were giving me; I just know they were good and I didn't feel a thing. I wish I had some of those right now!

For me, I was so out of it, I couldn't say anything. I was trying to say, "I don't want you guys in here right now." Then, they took the baby out of my arms.

Who did?

I think it was my mom. Mom grabbed him and I saw my baby being passed to all these people. I couldn't register it all. I think it was mom, then dad, then my grandfather, then my dad's dad, then my dad's girlfriend.

Oh, your grandparents were there then? I didn't know that.

Yes.

What were they saying to you?

They weren't saying anything to me. They didn't say anything.

They were sad and probably still in shock, Kerri. Maybe they thought that was the first and *last* time they would ever see that precious child. I can't imagine how hard that was for them. In the hospital, I wanted to be your mother and take care of you. What we needed was you, me, Jeff, Bryant, and the doctors and nurses and Mark and Terri. That would have been much easier.

It was great to have all my friends there, though.

Yes. They were sweet. They actually helped me a lot.

Once my family got done holding the baby, they put the baby back in my arms, and they left.

Well, Dr. T booted them out.

Yes! That was crazy! They left and you guys got to come in. I remember the first thing you said to me was, "Can I hold him?" and I remember thinking, *What the heck, Jody, he's your kid.*

You said, "Of course you can. He's your son." He was beautiful.

Yeah, he wasn't one of those weird crinkly babies. He was beautiful when he was born. He got taken away from me so fast by my family that my head kind of spun. I was like, *What just happened?* But for you guys to come in it meant a lot more to me than my family seeing him. Because he was *your* child. I wanted you to be part of the entire birthing experience. I wanted you to be in the delivery room. I know you wouldn't have had a single issue doing that.

No. I would have pushed him out if I could have! I would have done anything you asked and would have loved to be in the delivery.

That was originally the plan.

I understood.

I know that you would have been extremely focused on the baby but would have also been focused on me. I know you would have glanced at him, though!

Of course! Meeting Scotty was unreal. Seeing you with him was surreal. There you were and there he was and you two were just like Houston and me, eight years before. How did you feel when you saw me hold him?

Oh, I was excited. It was a great feeling. I don't want this to sound weird but it was a relief that it was finally over. I thought, *It's over, it's done with, he's out, he's with them. I don't have to worry anymore. Now all I have to worry about is the surrender process and coping with it.* I knew I had a whole new can of worms to open, but the main part of it was over.

The hard part, the delivery and the initial giving him to you, was done. A lot of the time right after him being born is hazy and foggy. I was on a lot of medicine.

Plus it was traumatic. You were in a lot of pain.

Yes, but I was just so happy it was over and I was so hungry. I just wanted to stop shaking and sleep. I went to sleep right after that. I needed to sleep and I slept for four or five hours. When I woke up later that night, Mom had gone home and I had a friend there. I was getting Dilaudid and Percoset. That first night I was pretty baked.

I would have taken him home right then if I could have, selfishly. But, I wanted to be there for you. I needed to be there. I felt like the nurses sometimes thought we were strange. I'm sure our situation was so open it surprised them. It felt like we were at St. Mary's a long time.

I was there for four days.

My favorite moment was that Saturday morning when just you, Scotty, and I were in my room. Nobody else was around. It was serene.

I remember that. The days leading up to you leaving were great.

I also remember that second day I got up out of bed and the first thing I wanted was a cigarette. I hadn't smoked a cigarette my whole pregnancy.

Who got the pack for you?

You did.

That's right! I don't smoke but I recognized the need.

That was the best cigarette of my life.

For a couple of days, we just passed Scotty back and forth down the hall. I wish our rooms had been side by side. I felt like, when I rolled by with him, the nurses thought I was nuts.

The nurses were great.

When we left, how were you? How would you describe the grieving process after we left the hospital and you went home?

The grieving process was a lot different than I thought it would be. The hardest day I had was the day he went home. That was the only day that I actually physically cried over it.

What helped you that day?

Nothing. There is nothing that can help you. I want to be really supportive to birthmothers: You can get through this, but there's going to be a day— it could be the day the baby's born, the day he goes home, a month later, a year later— there's going to be a day where you break down.

Or several days.

Or several. You will break down and cry and lose your mind. I had one day. I made people leave. I didn't want to be with anybody. I wanted to be by myself. After that, I was fine.

What about when you got home? Like, with your family?

I still had a friend there taking care of me. The problem was that my mom was devastated and mad at me.

Do you think she was mad or grieving? This was her grandson she lost.

Both.

All birthmothers grieve, all to different extents, but you handled everything better than I expected... What do you think made the biggest difference, what helped you get through those first few months of grief?

I think the fact that we are so open helped the most. And Bethany counselors were so good to me. Lauren prepared me.

And you knew you could still see Scotty.

Right. I didn't lose it as much as I thought I was going to. I thought all along, *I'm doing this and it's going to suck and I'm going to have a hard time and cry all the time,* but it really wasn't like that. Yes, I grieved and I was sad but I knew that I was going to be okay. I could see him and not worry.

Open adoption takes the edge off the emotional stress for both sides. It relieves a lot of the "fear of the unknown." In your opinion what are the pros of an open adoption?

One of the greatest things about an open adoption is that there isn't any mystery. You know what your baby is doing, where he is, what he looks like, how he's developing.

Don't you think that's really what most birthparents want to know?

They don't necessarily want to play catch or give him a bottle. They just want to know he's all right.

Don't get me wrong, I would totally play catch with Scotty in the backyard. But it's such a comfort when you know he's taken care of.

What are the cons of an open adoption? What are things that are hard about it?

Well, there have been times that I've wanted to see the baby.

And I've said no. There have been times I'm sure when I've let you down. How do you cope with that?

Yes, that kind of sucks. But, I'm an understanding person. I tell myself, *She's got a ten-year-old, a two-year-old, baseball, work, school, a husband; she's got stuff that's going on.* That's what I have to tell my family. They will ask, "Why can't she bring him over?" and I tell them you are a typical human being, that you've got other things to do besides wait on me to call you.

What would you tell adoptive parents? What advice would you give those who are worried about open adoption? Some are scared. They don't understand it or they are afraid it will be as open as ours and they don't want that.

The best thing to do is discuss with the birthmother how open you want the adoption to be. If she wants an open adoption like what we have, and you don't, then it's not going to work out, and you don't want to try to force something that's not going to work.

We had that little contract, which really wasn't legal, it was just a list of things to consider and agree upon.

I have it. Look at all these papers I kept.

Yep, here it is. You have it. Post-Placement Adoption Agreement. Oh my gosh. You've never been to our house and I wrote I would welcome you there.

No. I haven't.

Well, I'm not as welcoming as I promised in that moment, am I?

Ha!

We wrote basically the same answers to most of the questions. We agreed to have lots of communication, regardless.

That's what I wanted.

How did the adoption change you?

I never really had something that I would stand for before. Adoption changed the person that I am. I am stronger. I even speak in public now.

Yes, you've spoken to Bethany clients several times.

I was never really as passionate about anything before.

I think you are proud of what you did, and you should be. Most people are not as strong as you are.

I'm extremely proud and passionate about what I did. There's no reason to be ashamed of it.

How would you describe your relationship with Scotty now?

He's at the point where he's very clingy to you.

Is that weird for you?

It is weird because he looks like me, and he clings to you. It's funny when we go out in public, like when we went to lunch with my friend. I was playing with Scotty, and the waiter said to me, "Mommy, don't do that to him!" He recognized the resemblance but he didn't know the situation. Scotty's so young right now so we don't have any like, serious, relationship. I'm sure we will when he gets older. It will be much different as he grows up.

Kerri, what will you think if he doesn't want to have a relationship? He's going to be a little boy. Even with Houston, there are times I say "Go tell Grandmama thank you" or "Call Bop and tell her about your grade card" and he drags his feet. So in a few years when Scotty is ten years old like Houston and just wants to play basketball, ride around town with Jeff, and wear the same socks every day, he may not want to visit you much. How do you think you'll deal with that?

It's going to suck and I'm not going to like it too much.

I mean, if he's normal, he'll be avoiding me, too, at some point. Jeff and Houston leave me in the lurch all the time!

I know. If he's a normal boy, then eventually he'll be like, "Whatever, I don't know. I don't want to deal with that," and I know there will be a lot of other feelings there, too. He could have an abandonment complex. Who knows?

Well, we can just make him read this book!

Yeah, and we also have a scrapbook I made for him. So he'll know I love him. If he doesn't want to see me, we'll just continue the relationship through you and me. You can just tell me what he's up to. If he decides later on in life that he doesn't want me in his life, then I'll back away. No problem.

What would you like for the future to be like with Scotty? What's an ideal relationship for you?

To still be around when he grows up. To still be in his life.

To what extent?

To any extent. I don't care as long as I know him. I will be in his life as much as he wants me to be. Not in the sense that I will be there all the time. One day he's going to graduate. I'd love to be there for that. One day he's going to get married, and I would LOVE to be there for that. So, it's really just a matter of what he wants and needs.

If some people prefer closed adoptions, I completely understand. Open adoption is hard sometimes. I think what helps us is that you and I respect each other and we both want Scotty to be emotionally and mentally sound.

Exactly.

What else would you say to adoptive families who are reading this book?

When you are dealing with the birthmothers and going through the process, eventually you are going to get picked. It may not happen right away. It may happen twenty-four hours after you finish your paperwork or nine years after. It could be a while. You have to be extremely patient and wait. For every adoptive parent there is a birthmother out there who is perfectly matched who is meant to give her baby to you. Every single one of you. Be patient. Remember that birthmothers are going through this, too. Jody, you described adoption as "grieving in reverse." Well, birth moms are grieving in the proper order. A birthmother may be very cautious because you are going to raise her child. She knows it's coming. In nine months everything is going to change. Your body changes, even your hair changes when you are pregnant. It changes the very core of who you are. You don't really know where you are going or how you are going to feel. Most people go through their whole lives and don't experience something this intense.

It's a leap of faith for birthmothers, too, Kerri.

It's a hard thing to do. You are putting your trust in so many people. You are putting a baby in somebody's hands. You are giving your baby to someone. He's part of you.

I think the main thing that people can learn from you and me is not to be afraid.

Don't be afraid of adoption, or of open adoption.

Absolutely. You might do something out of your comfort zone and it might be an incredible experience.

It could be. I am a birthmother. I gave my son to you because I was not ready to be a mother, but I do want to be a mother. One of these days, I'm going to have my *own* baby.

Looking Back and Looking Forward

As I write this, my tow-headed Scotty is pulling family picture albums off a bookshelf and excitedly watching them slide to a pile on the floor. What a privilege it is to watch a child so longed for make a mess. My father often reminded me to enjoy the simple moments and tasks in life. My mother once said to me that the best days are the ones where nothing extreme happens. My parents said so because our time on Earth —we hope—consists mostly of these happy, ordinary days. As an adoptive mother who suffered the heartache of infertility and then undertook the rigorous requirements and torturous wait of the adoption journey, I assure you that I am perfectly content watching my child wreck the den.

When we started the adoption course, Jeff and I knew little about current day adoption. All we knew was Jeff and his parents' experience of a completely closed adoption. When we completed the "Openness Questionnaire" for Bethany, we agreed to any level from completely closed to open, not wanting to limit our opportunities. Open adoption (of any degree) can eliminate mystery for the adoptive parents, the child, and the birthparents. It is tough for me to navigate through decisions sometimes.

Now and then, I am a little jealous of my adoptive mother friends who have closed adoptions and no entanglements with birth families. However, when I consider our experience as a whole, I am happy to sacrifice time and energy in exchange for the unimaginable sacrifice Kerri, Bryant and *their* families made for Jeff, Houston, Scotty, and me. We communicate freely with one another, but I do not feel trapped or overly obligated. I usually try to speak to Kerri at least once a month on the phone. Our visits seem to be tapering off. Sometimes we go two to three months without seeing each other. When Kerri and I do visit, we typically spend an hour or so together. Houston comes, too. I do not want Scotty to feel any more different than necessary, and I want Houston to learn from and share the experience with his brother. I do get nervous when I plan a visit with Kerri and her family, not because I am uncomfortable around them, but because I still cannot fully grasp the magnitude of what she did for me. Scotty's adoption was an academic, emotional, and spiritual education beyond measure and I appreciate every moment of the sometimes-stormy journey. Our adoption is not "typical" but the emotional elements and lessons to be learned from our story are universal.

My "Smiling Boy" Scotty spends his days imitating Houston's basketball shots and batting stance. Houston adores Scotty. As he promised, Houston pushes Scotty in his stroller, swims with him, reads to him, and jumps around and makes his baby brother laugh. Scotty obsessively watches the Golf Channel. He wears snug Elmo pajamas while taking long, peaceful naps in the "museum to the *now known* child." He runs and scatters toys among adoring fans at ballgames and family parties. *Possum Come a Knockin'* is his favorite book and bananas are his favorite food. Scotty knows what the cow, owl, and dog say. He knows that he is loved.

Waiting parents, have confidence in your dream. Have confidence in your decisions. After all of those futile years at a fertility clinic, I gave up on trying to control my body. Jeff, Houston, and I embarked on the spiritually centered expedition that is adoption. After months of "thinking pink" and only a few days of soul-searching, I called Mark and said, "Check the boy box!" God told me "She is on her way" on July 4, 2009, and Kerri conceived Scotty in August.

Jeff and I met a stranger, listened to her story, and took a titanic leap of faith. For years, I thought daily of Proverbs 13:12, "Hope deferred maketh the heart sick: but when the desire cometh, it is a tree of life." Through fertility treatments and the challenges of adoption, my hopes were deferred, over and over again. But, with Kerri and Bryant's commitment, the intangible desire materialized in our very tangible sweet Scotty, a precious, tender branch on our family tree. We can hold the son and sibling for whom we worked and dreamed for eight years.

When our relationship with Kerri evolved toward an open adoption, I set a compass toward "erring on the side of Christian kindness" and braced myself for a voyage superior to what I had planned or expected. The intermittent calm I found in prayer sustained me. The calm was the promise of happiness to come. I now know many women who have weathered the adoption voyage, many of whom endured much more dramatic, heartbreaking twists and turns than I. Then again, some enjoyed the lightest of burdens and their children arrived seemingly overnight. I cannot tell you what your adoption journey will be; I can only promise it will be a journey unlike anything you can imagine.

Waiting families, soak up the dashed hopes, frustrations, stresses, humor, triumphs, and miracles that are the stormy currents of adoption. As needed, seek the calm eye of the storm through prayer, supportive counsel, and self-confidence. Know that what you are doing is right and good.

Soon enough, you will spend Heavenly, ordinary days with your child. Until then, embrace the enlightening, beautiful, burdens bound in *your* "journey of faith." BELIEVE.

Houston never doubted. He told his elementary school principal, "I'm getting a baby when I'm eight years old," and he did.

My mother recently asked Houston, now eleven years old, "Who do you love most in this world?"

Houston answered, "Scotty."

He stilled the storm to a whisper;
the waves of the sea were hushed.

—Psalm 107:29

Author's Notes

I pray that, throughout this story, I acknowledged everyone who helped my family. If I left you out, please forgive me, as I typed most of these pages before dawn while my family was asleep or around Houston and Jeff's fantasy football games and Scotty's Mickey Mouse Clubhouse episodes. I need to thank a few certain people.

First, I say THANK YOU to my mother, Donna Cantrell. You are a natural storyteller able to intuitively explain the human condition. You know precisely how to love and, lucky for me, precisely how to proofread! Your love and words are endless. Your compassion for others is unmatched. Thank you for everything imaginable.

Second, I express a multitude of gratitude to Christina Drill, my spirited, succinct editor, who understood everything I said, at the speed of which I said it! To this project, you applied your NYU education and your natural ability with heart and diplomacy. You, my dear, are a "festival of lights."

Third, Terri Bowles, of Bethany Christian Services, you are nicknamed "The Closer" for a reason. Thank you for being with Kerri in the hospital and guiding her gently and lovingly, still.

Fourth, I thank my exceptional in-laws, Jeff and Jane Dyer, for leading by example, in adoption, in marriage, and in loving others.

Fifth, Houston and Scotty, I appreciate you beyond measure. I am in awe of your innocent and pure love for each other and I thank you for inspiring me and entertaining me every day. *I love you as much as a mother can love.*

Finally, Jeff, as I declared when you proposed, you are a dream come true. Who knew we would share two more dreams in our children? Thank you for understanding me. Thank you for posting up and playing hard all the way to the buzzer for me, for Houston, for Scotty, and for Kerri.

I used many quotations in this book, which may seem odd to avid readers who are accustomed to seeing one or two literary references in an entire novel. A typical author may use only one epitaph to set the mood at the beginning of a piece of work or each of its chapters. I wanted my readers to have more. If you consider a lengthy experience (highs and lows, moments of despair, humor, and inspiration), you should recognize that music, poetry, literature, movies, and assorted other "phrases" frame moments comprising that experience. We humans build each other up and color each other's lives with commentary and art. Waiting mothers and fathers need every emotional resource available—even cliché's—to help them tread the torrents of adoption.

Journalism, music, politics, and literature are businesses composed of intellectual property. Thus, rights are protected. When I completed the creative job of writing this story, I began the systematic, scrutinizing job of formatting pages and crediting sources for my quotes. I looked through countless books in this genre, which I *think* is narrative non-fiction, only to find no definitive "how-to" on citing quote sources. My school's librarian indulged me with guidance and examples of similar books, my bookshelves at home emptied their contents, the internet aided and confused me, and my diligent, prodigy of an editor did some "extensive digging" only to surmise that the new frontier of self-publishing has made such citation "wishy-washy." I could roll the dice and simply credit sources as they appeared, or hedge my bets and cite sources. As a humble wage-earning public school teacher, I chose to CMA to the best of my ability. References are listed in alphabetical order by author's last name.

References:

Austen, J. (2010). *Persuasion*. London: Arcturus.

Bethany Christian Services. (2012). Retrieved from
    http://www.bethany.org/

BibleGateway.com. (2012). Retrieved from
    http://www.biblegateway.com/

BrainyQuote.com. (2012). Retrieved from
    www.brainyquote.com

Burg, M. & Iotarpas, C. (Producers), & Evans, D. (Director).
    (1993). *The sandlot* [Motion picture]. United States: 20th
    Century Fox.

Burns, R. (1993). *Robert Burns : selected poems*. London New
    York: Penguin Books.

Carroll, L. (2005). *Alice's adventures in Wonderland; &
    Through the looking-glass*. New York: Spellbinder.

Charbonnet, P. (Producer), & Gray, F. (Director). (1995).
    Friday [Motion picture]. United States: New Line Cinema.

Coehlo, P. (2005). *Eleven minutes*. New York: Perennial.

Conroy, P. (2005). *The prince of tides*. New York: Dial Press
    Trade Paperbacks.

Davis, B. (1962). *The lonely life*. New York: G. P. Putnam's Sons.

DiPiero, B. & Tillis, P. (1991). *Melancholy child*. On *Put yourself in my place*.
    [Cassette]. United States: Arista Records.

Farlex, Inc. (2012). *The free dictionary by farlex*. Retrieved from
    http://www.thefreedictionary.com/

Lindhome, R. & Micucci, K. (2009). *Pregnant women are smug*. On *Music
    songs*. [CD]. United States: Amazon Digital Services.

Leroux, G. (2007). *The phantom of the opera*. New York: Barnes & Noble Books.

Lewis, C. (2001). *A grief observed*. San Francisco: HarperSanFrancisco.

Lipman, E. (1990). *Then she found me*. New York: Washington Square Press.

Milne, A. (2011). *Winnie-the-Pooh*. SanRafael, Calif: Ishi Press International.

Moncur, M., & QuotationsPage.com. (2012). The quotations page. Retrieved from http://www.quotationspage.com

Moore, L. (2010). *A gate at the stairs : a novel*. New York, N.Y: Vintage Books.

Seuss. (1990). *Oh, the places you'll go!* New York: Random House.

Shakespeare, W (1993). *Macbeth*. New York: Dover Publications.

Shakespeare, W. (2004). *The tragedy of Richard III*. New York: Washington Square Press.

Wells, R. (2002). *Divine secrets of the Ya-Ya Sisterhood*. New York, NY: HarperTorch.

Williams, T. (1999). *The glass menagerie*. New York: New Directions.

Woolf, V. (1991). *A room of one's own*. New York: Harcourt Brace Jovanovich.

Woolf, V. (2006). *The waves*. Orlando, Fla: Harcourt.

Yeats, W. (2009). *Responsibilities*. Whitefish, MT: Kessinger.

Yeats, W. (2002). *The Yeats reader : a portable compendium of poetry, drama, and prose*. New York: Scribner Poetry.